*A booster for self-esteem and personal
fulfillment, this book is also the story
of one person's humorous and practical
insights into finding significance and
meaning in the retirement years.*

*Really living life all the way
in the later years requires
neither money or perfect health—
just an excitement about the future,
a desire to keep going and a faith in God.*

Fill Your Days With Life

by <u>MILDRED VANDENBURGH</u>

A Division of G/L Publications
Glendale, California, U.S.A.

The Authorized Version (*KJV*) is the basic
Bible version used in this book. Other
Bible version:
   RSV, Revised Standard Version, copyrighted 1946
   and 1952 by the Division of Christian Education
   of the NCCC, U.S.A., and used by permission.

Published by
Regal Books Division, G/L Publications
Glendale, California 91209, U.S.A.

Library of Congress Catalog Card No. 74-16964
ISBN 0-8307-0323-3

The publishers do not necessarily endorse the entire
contents of all publications referred to in this book.

CONTENTS

Respectfully dedicated to
David T. MacKerron
Organizer and Sponsor of the JOLLY SIXTIES
First Baptist Church of Van Nuys, California

FOREWORD

Experience is the greatest teacher! Even to the casual observer this is an obvious fact. And it is from this vantage point that Mildred Vandenburgh writes. What she has to say concerning older adults and the Jolly Sixties program in our church is something she has experienced; she has lived it and, as she so ably points out in the text, she has loved every minute of it.

Her purpose in presenting this volume to the reading public is not only to entertain, but to inspire. Doctors are becoming more and more proficient in the science of geriatrics. Consequently, life is being prolonged. Retired people by the thousands are looking for things

1

to do. The church has a tremendous opportunity for ministry among them—a ministry that results in souls being saved, the elimination of loneliness, and a challenge for service.

The Jolly Sixties are a mighty army for God. Even though our annual budget is over $2,000,000, we do not have enough money to pay for the nitty-gritty jobs they do for Christ in the course of a year. I, therefore, would like to join Mildred in urging every evangelical church to launch its own Senior Adult program.

Harold L. Fickett, Jr., Pastor
First Baptist Church of Van Nuys
Van Nuys, California

AUTHOR'S PREFACE

Words fail me in attempting to express my gratitude to all the nice individuals, editors and publishers, from Bethlehem to Brazil, who graciously responded to my queries and requests by supplying me with information, photos, printed matter, permissions to quote, along with their prayers and encouragement. It was worth all of the labor, the travail, perplexities and vicissitudes of putting a book together to make or renew their acquaintances.

If I have been amiss or unable to contact anyone I have quoted, I hereby express my regrets and shall gladly incorporate proper credit in future editions of my book if he will contact the editorial staff.

To Dollie Reed and other Jolly Sixties who ransacked trunks and files for negatives, records, diaries and reminders I say, "Thank you! Thank you!" To staff members of the First Baptist Church of Van Nuys for reviewing various chapters, to Dr. Fickett for writing the Preface, to Mrs. Fickett for reading and commending the entire manuscript, and to my daughter Portia Gribble, a writer and editor in her own right, for keeping me on the track, I am deeply indebted.

Most grateful of all am I to my loving Lord, who met me at the breakfast table each morning and directed my eyes and my fingers to His words most applicable to the day's topics; who awakened me at all times of the night with ideas which otherwise would not have occurred to me; and who transformed my fidgety nerves and flighty fingers into instruments of calm and composure. For God is not the author of confusion, but of peace (1 Cor. 14:33).

AGING DEFLATES THE EGO

Choir practice was over and we were putting the music back in our folders. A warm, exuberant feeling swept over me. At last I could enjoy again the harmony and fellowship of blending my voice with the voices of other Christians in singing praises to the Lord.

For a number of years grading papers and making lesson plans had demanded my weekday evenings. My own children needed me to supervise their homework, too. A mother shouldn't leave four lively youngsters alone week after week to attend choir practice. And they were too old for baby-sitters.

Now they were grown up, and I was through teaching school. This was my first evening back in a choir loft. Too bad I had arrived late. The director was new and I hadn't met him personally. I'd slipped quietly into the soprano section. No problem! I had directed choirs and glee clubs myself, and reading music was a cinch.

5

I didn't expect solo parts at first. I was willing to volunteer my expertise to choral work until I got back "in voice."

Then the bombshell burst! The director was urging members to be regular in attendance. "If the Lord has given you a voice, you owe it to Him and the church to be faithful. I know you are busy people. But don't drop out and expect to come back when it is convenient. Voices change when you don't use them. Trying to join up after you're forty doesn't work out. Be in your robes at 10:45 Sunday morning. Let us pray."

I didn't hear his prayer. All I heard was "after you're forty." This wasn't a youth choir. Several were in their forties. I knew them personally. Most had never had a voice lesson in their lives. The tenor in back of me sang soprano all evening. The young woman on my left sharped so badly I had to sing with all my might to keep her on pitch. None of them had my training. Not even the director, I suspected. I had graduated from Baylor University in voice and continued my training with D. A. Clippinger and Louis Graveur. I had my master's degree in music from the University of Southern California. I'd sung in big-time light opera companies and in summer stock.

After you're forty? The very idea! I bit my lip to stop its quivering and hurried into my raincoat.

The other members were kind. They didn't stare at me. They just walked out.

I dashed to my car in a downpour and headed for home.

"Over forty! Over forty!" my windshield wipers rasped in mocking rhythm.

I slowed them down. Water drenched the windshield and blocked my view.

"Can't sing! Can't sing!" the wipers groaned.

Tears of self-pity and anger streaming down my face and the deluge outside caused me to almost miss my driveway. I slammed on the brakes to make the turn. The car swerved and banged against the garage door, broadside. The motor died, and there I sat, without the slightest inclination to praise the Lord in song.

My sobs were crescendoing into fortissimo when a flashlight beamed through the window. My neighbor had heard the crash. He was a kind man and always ready to help. I had to be civil and lower the glass.

"Your garage must have shrunk in the rain," he drawled. "Try approaching it from another angle. I'll open the door for you if you'll move over."

The sobs in my throat gurgled into a giggle.

"This old Rambler has rammed its last rumble tonight," I told him. "I'm leaving it right here and going to bed."

"Why not?" he agreed. "It can't get any wetter. The sun may be shining in the morning. Cheer up!"

And he was gone.

Swan Song Blues

The next morning my eyes were red and swollen. "You look like sixty," I told the face in the mirror, "but your

7

voice couldn't sound like sixty. Your lyric soprano couldn't phase out that badly. Maybe you are too sensitive. Maybe Mr. Wilbur wasn't referring to you. I'll prove you can still sing."

I got out my tape recorder, sat down at the piano, and accompanied myself on Handel's "Come unto Me" from the *Messiah*. The playback was a traumatic revelation. My attacks on high F sounded like assaults. My slurs were skids. Sustained tones had a pronounced tremolo. Diction was muddled. In spots, I committed the unpardonable sin. I flatted!

The shock knuckled me under. My lyric soprano days were over. I had allowed my most treasured gift from God to deteriorate by neglect. I was the slothful servant who buried my talent in the ground. Teaching songs to school children and vocalizing while driving to and from work were the only opportunities I had to sing for a long time.

On second thought, I didn't have to stop singing altogether. Voices generally settle into the speaking range when sopranos and tenors neglect vocal exercises. I could move down into the contralto register and support the alto section!

Hopefully, I faced the microphone again and sang the low version of the same aria, "He Shall Feed His Flock." Tones came easier. My voice seemed velvety and resonant. But alas! The playback was like the Ugly Queen's "Mirror, mirror on the wall." My tones were breathy and wobbly. The five-note slur on "shep" was spotty and chopped up. Cracked? Oh, no!

I ran the tape again. It sounded worse than the first time. Those unscheduled stops between tones *were* cracks!

I opened another box of Kleenex and had a heart-to-heart talk with the has-been who used to be me.

"You would have been a better influence on your children if you had never phased out on choir work. You might have preserved your voice, old woman. You didn't prepare for retirement. You just let it swoop down on you. Now you have nothing but leaves to offer the Lord. You've let your music training go down the drain. Get out your knitting needles."

New Hope

I was in the lowest of spirits when an old friend, Bea Shepard, phoned me. She told me she was the program chairman for the Jolly Sixties' socials at the First Baptist Church of Van Nuys, a Los Angeles suburb in the San Fernando Valley, home of 1,500,000 people.

"I had an old-timers home talent program prepared for next Tuesday night, but my feature soloist is down with the flu. How about bringing your harmonica and filling in for me?" she asked.

"Who are the Jolly Sixties?" I grumbled sourly.

"Our senior adult organization at the church," she replied. "They organized in 1960 for Christian fellowship and service, so they call themselves the Jolly Sixties."

"I don't qualify," I moped. "I'm not jolly, and I feel

9

more like ninety than sixty." Yet being wanted was a lift.

"I don't care how old you feel," Bea retorted. "You'll get out of your doldrums if you get with us. That's what we're all about. Come on now, and help me out. Your harmonica will fit perfectly in this type of program."

"I'd feel like a fool tooting a mouth organ before strangers in that big church," I hesitated.

"They're never strangers. The socials are in the gym. And I want you to play like a fool. It's all in fun. Don't let me down. Dish up a package of old ditties and dig some old clothes out of your closet. I'll come by for you at seven o'clock."

I sensed the friendly atmosphere when I stepped into the gymnasium. Everybody called each other by first names. Costumes ranged from pantalets to bustles, from knee pants to overalls.

The program opened with four couples on stage in a square dance routine. Next, a trio did a lively package of hillbilly hoedowns on a washtub bass, piano, and fiddle played left-handed on the lap. My inhibitions vanished. I played old favorites for fifteen minutes while everybody sang along or clapped in rhythm.

During the social period after the program, some who had played harmonicas suggested a band. Others wanted to learn. Bea introduced me to Dave MacKerron, the youthful sponsoring minister, whom they all call "Dave."

"Our church has hobby classes Monday evenings," he said. "I think a harmonica class would go over big. In fact I'll join it myself."

10

That evening with the Jolly Sixties completely changed my outlook on life. Here were men and women in my category who not only accepted the fact of ageness—they were enjoying it! The hard-of-hearing didn't try to cover up. They asked people to speak up. The blind and partially blind were guided into the refreshment line and briefed on varieties of desserts from which to choose. Cups in shaky hands were not filled to the brim. Friends took refreshments to those in wheelchairs.

Dave could induce a spirit of reverence by prayer, hymn singing and devotionals, then shift to hilarity by donning a wig and ridiculous costume and singing in falsetto with exaggerated gestures. I got the feeling he was sort of a son-image to the old folk he so energetically lifted to a plane of abandonment.

Submission

Instead of talking to myself when I got home, I got down on my knees for advice.

"Lord, did You send my old friend to lift me from self-pity to realization? Are You humbling me by expecting me to adapt my music background to a simple organ of Jubal? People look down their noses at the mouth organ and at people who take it seriously. Can I bear that? And how could a harmonica group serve You in a big church with the highest of music standards? What kind of music could we play to Your glory? Should I transfer my membership to this church? Is this Your plan for my retirement service?"

The answer wasn't immediate. Other questions bothered me. How long could a person schooled in classical music revel in such ditties as "Oh! Susanna" and "Billy Boy"? Would oldsters have enough breath to blow and draw on harmonicas? Would blowing and inhaling pull dentures loose? In almost any adult class, dropouts are to be expected. But would this one *fizzle* out?

Bea urged me on. "What harm if it's just a fly-by-night thing if it gives a few people happiness? Harmonicas aren't expensive. There's little to lose if we just do a stunt or two at socials."

"I'm not a good loser," I confessed. "Once I start something, I hate to give it up."

"I don't think you'll have to. If Dave backs it, it's sure to succeed. In the meantime, get acquainted with the group. Come to the Friday morning Bible class. Go with me to the next monthly birthday dinner at the Ontra Cafeteria. And let's go together on our next bus trip to Knott's Berry Farm. I'll make the reservations."

That sounded like good advice and a lot of good fellowship. Something a has-been of sixty-five needs very much.

BIRTHDAYS AND BUSES

2

It was noon on the last Sunday of the month, and the lineup at the Ontra Cafeteria extended onto the sidewalk outside. Strangers and regular patrons were not long in discovering that the two to three hundred jovial, bantering and vivacious oldsters who encompassed them fore and aft were the Jolly Sixties. These folk had lost no time in evacuating the sanctuary, forming car pools, and driving the three-mile distance to the festive rendezvous.

Cafeteria employees and members of the "Jolly" birthday committee waited beside checkers' registers to carry trays for the frail, the crippled and the blind to the private dining room reserved for the gala occasion. Those with birthdays or wedding anniversaries that month were ushered to a central table festooned with

streamers and flowers by the committee who had attended the early church service in order to have all in readiness when the crowd arrived. They poured coffee and cut and served the jumbo birthday cake which was furnished by the cafeteria.

When the decorated cake was brought in from the kitchen and held up for view, Dave signaled for all present to salute the feted ones with the song, "Happy Birthday (or Anniversary) to You." For these happy people, the concept of another year gone by is not one of adversity, but of joy and gratitude to the Lord; especially for "bonus years" beyond three score and ten.

On this occasion, a ninety-year-old member and a couple celebrating their fifty-fifth wedding anniversary were given special honors.

Some of the 1500 on the mailing list who look forward to notices about monthly birthday dinners, socials, and bus trips are affiliated with other churches without such programs; others are with various cults, and some with no religious organization whatever. These outreaches, where non-Christians rub shoulders with the devout who are praying for them, are open doors to the way of salvation. Great is the rejoicing when one enters in.

Observing the joy and fellowship I wondered how many of these people might have spent "their day" alone, with perhaps a card or two to remind them they were growing old, were it not for a church that cares. Yet these dinners cost the church nothing, nor do the socials or bus trips.

The offerings taken at socials cover costs of refreshments, entertainment, mailing expense, and pay for memorial books, tapes and filmstrips that are donated to the church library in memory of deceased members. They also purchase gifts of appreciation for outstanding service, and for incidentals. On monthly bus trips, "love offerings" or a small addition to admission fees (at special rates) defray the cost of gasoline. These bus trips may be to the Dodgers Stadium, Forum, Music Center, Ice Follies, County Fair at Pomona, Date Festival at Indio, Art Festival at Laguna Beach, boat trips to Catalina Island or whatever else Dave's fertile imagination conjures up for his gadabouts.

Many participants have given up driving because of their failing eyesight, heart condition, or slowed-down reaction time incompatible with freeway momentum. Retirees from beaches and inland towns come to the Valley to ride with the Jolly Sixties. For the recluse gripped by agoraphobia—an exaggerated fear of venturing away from home—these bus trips are of therapeutic value.

A few years ago when the church needed an additional bus, the Jolly Sixties negotiated the purchase by collecting 3400 books of trading stamps.

Drivers of church buses are staff members or firemen, insurance agents, and self-employed who donate their services. These men must qualify with a special state license, minimum and maximum age limit, physical examination, and classroom and behind-the-wheel training by the staff transportation director of bus ministry. They transport people of all ages to Sunday School, rallies, weekend camps and retreats, family outings, sports events, choir and missionary outreach tours, vacation day-camp trips, teachers institutes, and convalescent hospitals.

Terry, the transportation director, told me the Jolly Sixties' monthly trips are the most exciting of all. I asked him why. "You get a different viewpoint from ours," he replied. "You're inside looking out. We're outside looking in."

Hesitantly, I asked him what he saw, bracing myself for some old generation-gap aphorism.

"My grandfather lived with our family, and I grew

16

up with him as a companion," Terry reminisced. "He stimulated my interest in the past. In his latter days he told me to watch out for the old devil, for he never lets you go, no matter what your age. As a youth, I wondered how a feeble, bedridden, elderly person could be tempted. 'Old Satan tries to get me to feel sorry for myself,' was his explanation. 'Don't ever feel sorry for yourself, my boy. Keep on praising the Lord for His goodness, and the devil will flee.' "

A positive attitude toward aging is rubbing off on these young men who transport us. Being with old people is nostalgic for Terry. "Before long, meeting people born in the nineteenth century will be a rare experience," he reflected. I'm sure he wasn't intentionally predicting my doom.

Every year, several trips to tourist sites such as Death Valley, Yosemite, the Grand Canyon, San Diego, and northern California are scheduled by chartered buses. In 1971, over forty Jollies cruised the Inside Passage to Alaska. And they have taken three flights to Hawaii.

3 THE BLIND LEAD THE WAY

For several months I was a two-timer, attending Sunday services at my home church and enjoying weekday activities at the other. With twenty-five churches of the same denomination in the Valley, shuttling is not unusual. I liked our minister and enjoyed the adult Sunday School class. I crawled from beneath my juniper tree and prayed away all ill feeling toward the choir director. An innate sense of humor flushed out my self-pity and enabled me to laugh at myself. My graduation recital in voice took place forty-five years ago. The operas I sang in were Victor Herbert's, and he died in 1924.

That soprano voice in the church choir still sounded sharp to me, but I could be wrong. A hearing test revealed a loss in my upper register. Though restless, I remained a seat warmer. No mighty wind, earthquake or fire projected me to where the action was. But a still, small voice kept asking, "What are you doing here?"

The first regular Friday morning Bible class for Jolly Sixties, which I visited, almost nudged me over. The hour opened with prayer requests and individual reports about visits to bereaved, accident victims, sick members, and shut-ins. (Some of the lay people who spend a day each week calling upon visitors, new members and shut-ins are Jolly Sixties. These devoted Christians each accept eight to ten names of members no longer able to be active, and call upon them once or twice a month to chat, read the Bible, share literature, and pray with them.)

A series of lessons on Revelation was being taught by an associate pastor, the Rev. Ed Kriz. Under Pastor Ed's tutelage, the Friday class attendance had tripled. "Teaching the class is a real challenge because of their eagerness to better discern this profound Book," he told me. He pointed out "one dear lady" so crippled with arthritis it took her twenty minutes to shuffle one block to the church. Yet she attended the class regularly and refused rides because she needed the exercise.

Pastor Ed's scholarship and spiritual leadership started me looking up cross references and comparing numerous Bible translations at the breakfast table. Aroused from my years of Laodiceanism, my study at first was like cramming for a final. Gradually the very words I was reading resolved my tension. As a result, I formed a habit of spending forty to sixty minutes with the Lord at breakfast. These daily devotions not only increased my knowledge and understanding of the Bible, but composed my compulsions for the day. Before long I could say like King David, "My voice shalt thou hear in the morning, O Lord; in the morning will I direct my prayer unto thee, and will look up" (Ps. 5:3).

Called into Service

It was the minister of the church's Blind Department who led me to a point of decision to transfer my membership. The Rev. Walther Olsen phoned to ask if I would substitute as pianist for the blind Sunday School class for a month during the absence of Dick Smith their regular pianist.

Dick is a blind concert pianist and keyboard virtuoso who teaches music at the Braille Institute in Los Angeles. Me substitute for him? My fingers were as stiff as my vocal cords, my thumbs bent by arthritis. Anyhow, I always attended my own church on Sundays.

Rev. Olsen had no inclination to proselyte. The decision had to be mine. I promised to fill in the following Sunday. That promise set me back on my piano bench an hour or more each day. I practiced scales and exercises to limber up and found it excellent therapy for my hands. I attempted to improvise on familiar tunes, for which Dick was noted. Unlike my enervated ears, the piano keys had absolute pitch—provided I struck the right ones! Day by day I made progress.

Once the routine was established, I continued daily practice until I could perform for my own satisfaction the Chopin, Liszt, Brahms, and Debussy selections I had learned in my teens. I even played them from memory!

Sad to say, memorizing new music was more difficult. Was it because my brain had shrunk? my metabolic rate was reduced? my heart pumped less blood to my brain? or, because there was a shortage of ribonucleic acid in my nerve cells? Any of these theories might explain my inaptitude. But I wasn't interested in proving a theory of gerontology. I was discovering that when God closes one door, He opens another.

A warm Christian fellowship was evident that Sunday morning among the blind, their teacher, and the many volunteers who transported and assisted the blind members.

After the opening song service I slipped into the Berean class—one of eight in the Jolly Sixties Department. Their teacher, the Rev. Dale Scott, was to play a vital role in my activities at the church.

At the 11:00 A.M. worship service I was lifted to new heights by the singing of the choir. The minister expounded the Scripture with flawless diction I could understand. Then and there I resolved to settle my double allegiance. I wanted to dedicate my remaining years to God in hope of compensating for the years I had been too busy, busy. Already, I had seen that I could be of service here.

Furthermore, the program this church provides would totally minister *to me* the rest of my life! If my eyesight should fail, the library would loan me talking books and Braille literature. When no longer able to drive, volunteers would transport me to church. If I should lose my remaining fifty percent hearing acuity, the Deaf

Department will teach me to "hear" through the intriguing gestures of sign language interpreters. Break my hip or suffer a stroke? Visitation ministers and members of the Extension Department would keep me in touch. One of the ministers would officiate at my funeral and my Christian associates would be bused to my interment. There would be no separation from Christian fellowship in life or in death.

At the end of the service during the closing invitation, I responded and presented myself as a candidate for church membership. I was assigned to a warm and friendly woman counselor who asked about my Christian experience. I opened up and revealed my peaks and ravines.

Missions and Music

"My Christian experience has been divided into three chapters," I replied. "My father was a deacon and my mother a Sunday School teacher as far back as I can recall. Mother's father was a Baptist preacher in a little town in Iowa. My father's mother lived with our family. Grandma read Bible stories and Sunday School papers to us children by the hour. As a child, I experienced nothing but a Christian atmosphere except when I visited in the home of a playmate whose family was different. Shocked at my first meal as a guest when the family ate without returning thanks, I ran home to my mother who explained that they were not Christians and we must pray for them. My love for Jesus and concern for unsaved friends were stimulated at my mother's knee. I was baptized when I was eight years old.

"My second chapter took place while I was a student at Baylor University. An elderly cousin of my grandfather, Dr. Henry Clay Mabie, gave a series of lectures on missions in the Orient. Dr. Mabie had served as corresponding secretary of the American Baptist Missionary Union for eighteen years. His story of his first tour of mission fields in China in 1891, nine years before the Boxer uprising, so engrossed me I responded to an appeal for dedication to go anywhere the Lord wanted me to go. But the school staff ignored me. More advanced students with higher qualifications made commitments that day. My inferiority complex convinced me I was unworthy. I was called but not chosen.

"With my call aborted, Christian service became a sideline while I studied, worked, raised a family, and lived as though a witch were leering over my shoulder, sweeping me from one day into the next. I directed my first church choir in my hometown before I was twenty. After moving to California, I led a choir in Alhambra for several years, and later, trained harmonica choirs of juniors in two Los Angeles churches.

"Now suddenly, upon retirement, I find myself on the threshold of a new day. Here in this church I experience fellowship, love, and evidence of respect and worthiness of the individual. In this atmosphere I'd like to open a new chapter in my book of life. My tithe will be only half of what it was before I retired. My assets are good health, what time the Lord grants me,

23

and a resolution to put God first, people second, and things last. My bonus years are the Lord's," I concluded.

The lady had listened with patience, then said; "We are truly a service organization. I am sure the Lord has work for you to do here. Shall we ask Him to help you find it?"

We concluded our conference with prayer.

Putting the older generation out to pasture was not a part of the culture of God's chosen people. The ancient Hebrew patriarch was head of his family and owner of his property until his death. But the theme song in many American homes today is "Granny doesn't live here any more"—by choice or by force. Family life is so mobile and disintegrated, grandparents don't fit into the chaos. Nor do they wish to be burdens to their children. Less than a quarter of the people sixty-five and over live with their children.

The significance of mass retirement has not kept pace with its reality, and gerontology is a relatively new science. Odds, generally chalked up against retirees, relate to fixed incomes, health, housing, nutrition, transportation and leisure time. Spiritual leaders who probe beneath materialism say retirees' needs are common to all, though perhaps accentuated by age: love, status, companionship, fun, a useful place in society, faith in God and assurance of eternal life.

The Rev. Paul W. Brauer, retired Lutheran minister, coined a slogan for his senior adult Sunday School class in Florida: Don't retire—aspire! "What a vast reservoir of time, talents and experience the Lord has given His church in the members who are retired!" he declared. "What a tremendous amount of good could be accomplished if we always knew how to channel their abilities into productive avenues for God and for society."[1]

It is doubtful if any one church has explored all of the channels in which retirees can be of service, or all of the services the church can render to uplift their spirits. On these points the Bible provides basic precepts.

Spiritual ministry is emphasized in Proverbs 18:14: "The spirit of a man will sustain his infirmity; but a wounded spirit who can bear?"

Paul told the Thessalonians to "Comfort yourselves together, and edify one another" (1 Thess. 5:11). Lonely people must be brought together in an environment conducive to consolation and edification.

They need a pervasive role in the church program. "Those that be planted in the house of the Lord shall flourish in the courts of our God. They shall still bring forth fruit in old age" (Ps. 92:13,14). Solomon says, "The hoary head is a crown of glory, if it be found in the way of righteousness" (Prov. 16:31).

The Jolly Sixties Story

The First Baptist Church of Van Nuys has always been a fundamental, Christ-centered, Bible-oriented church. When Dr. Harold L. Fickett, Jr., accepted the pastorate in 1959, he brought with him a conviction that each individual is precious in the sight of God. He visualized a ministry adapted to all who look to the church for fellowship and Christian leadership: the deaf, the blind, the paraplegic, youth, and especially the aging founders of the church and the increasing number of senior adults moving into the San Fernando Valley.

Dr. Fickett, Sr., is a constant reminder to his son that an abundant life need not be terminated by a date line, and he is a living example of dynamic maturity to older church members. "Dad Fickett" retired at age sixty-five from a twenty-five year pastorate of a church in Texas, whose membership numbered 3000. Now he says he never really retired—he was retread! He has averaged 124 sermons a year preaching in Spain, Italy, Germany, Hawaii, Massachusetts, Texas and California. At present, he is serving as interim pastor for a church in Texas.

"Dad Fickett" had been alone ever since his wife passed away in 1964. At eighty-three, he sent for his son to marry him to a vivacious and amiable Texas widow.

Some twenty-five years ago a heart attack taught him to eat properly, keep his mind active, and keep busy without overtaxing his strength. To this formula he adds: "Keep in touch with friends. Retain interest in

27

the Lord's work and in His people. Take time off occasionally to go fishing. And keep looking to the future."

At four-score and five, what a motto!

Pastor Fickett brought with him to the West Coast David MacKerron, a young and energetic graduate from Boston University, gifted in music and drama, and skilled in physical fitness. Dave was experienced in youth leadership and had done field work in gerontology. Designating him as minister of weekday activities, Dr. Fickett gave him a choice of specializing in youth or senior adult leadership. Dave chose the latter. Fifteen years later, he is still happy with his decision. So are the Jolly Sixties.

To activate a program for senior adults at Van Nuys Baptist, a meeting was called late in 1959 for all who were interested. Twelve responded. They selected officers, adopted the name, "Jolly Sixties," planned a social calendar and service projects, opened membership to anyone from fifty years up, regardless of church affiliation.

Social and Service Activities

Monthly socials are now attended by about 500 persons. The agenda starts with gospel songs, welcome to visitors, business, and a devotional. An art committee sets up decorations and stage settings in keeping with skits, musicales, travel slides, or seasonal programs staged by a program committee. Outside talent is often booked to wind up the entertainment. Refreshments are served at the close of the program or a potluck precedes it. The dinners draw the largest attendance.

Monthly dinners in a private dining room of a cafeteria originated with a surprise birthday dinner for Dave about twelve years ago. That same year, Dave initiated monthly bus trips by driving a church bus with thirty-two "Jollies" to Disneyland.

The original Sunday School class ballooned into a department with one men's, three women's, and four mixed classes, each with its own officers. Dave MacKerron is the superintendent.

Forty to fifty men and women stay after Friday morning Bible class each week and put in about 3000 work hours per year, which relieves the church of much labor and expense. Their project is the final preparation of 7000 church bulletins for Sunday worship services. Sometimes other printed materials are brought for them to sort, assemble and staple. These same volunteers also assemble blood packets for the Red Cross once a month, mend choir music, and help in the print shop.

(Those with arthritic fingers have discovered that skimming off single sheets from a stack of papers is good therapy, like picking up marbles with your toes to strengthen the arches.)

At noon they have coffee. Some bring sandwiches. All enjoy chit-chatting as they work. They look forward to this Friday fellowship and the opportunity to be of service, and the church staff is confident the job will be done, rain or shine. To these Jolly Sixties, Friday is another Lord's day.

Jolly Sixties also handle special and bulk mailings, an on-call service not on a regular schedule. A crew is on call to serve meals at the church. Meals are served in several areas, from the social hall next to the kitchen to the fifth floor in the Youth Center.

Vacation Bible School transforms the church kitchen into a beehive of "Jollies" counting out cookies and pouring punch to be served mid-morning to hundreds of children.

On Monday evenings some 200 trained volunteers

report to Rev. John DeSaegher, a visitation minister, for dinner and assignments. They fan out, two by two, and each couple makes an average of four calls upon people who signed visitors' cards at worship services, upon new members who have not become involved, and upon unresolved seekers. Rev. DeSaegher believes these stimulating contacts add years to the lives of the Jolly Sixties involved in the visitation ministry. The legendary woodman who cuts his own firewood is said to be twice warmed. These people are *thrice* warmed. They have dinner out and spend the evening with a congenial companion. They serve the Lord and their church. And they invite new friends into their circle.

Consecrated seniors are among other specially trained church members engaged in a "one-to-one discipleship ministry." They go to homes of new converts and give them a series of lessons on Bible study and church doctrine.

It was a retired couple who planted the seed from which the church's Extension Department germinated. Bill and Myrtle formed a habit of calling regularly upon the elderly who were forced by a handicap to drop out from church attendance. The Extension Department has since become a vital ministry, reaching workers employed on Sundays as well as the handicapped.

Because members of the Blind Department are scattered from Hollywood to San Fernando, transportation by church buses is not generally feasible. Senior adults are among volunteer drivers who have been bringing the blind to church ever since their department was initiated in 1963. They also transport them to a bowling alley once a week, to handbell choir practice Saturday mornings, to social events, and on personal errands.

When special needs arise, Jolly Sixties respond whole-heartedly. One instance was the stringing of thousands of beads between metal chain links on eight great crystal chandeliers for the new sanctuary. These chandeliers shine as memorials to strained eyesight and pricked and blistered fingers.

Another such instance was ministry to victims of the 1971 earthquake in our Valley. Church members, from junior high work crews on up, contributed toward physical, material, and spiritual needs of families whose homes were damaged or demolished. One dedicated couple, who regularly counsels new converts at Sunday services, made ninety-one visits in the devastated area taking food, clothing and Bibles, and sharing Campus Crusade's "Four Spiritual Laws." Through it all, Mr. and Mrs. Fred King led fifty-two persons to Christ.

Though they form a special department, older church members are not segregated from missionary circles, men's fellowship, the board of deacons, ushering, and various Sunday School and child care services. They coach athletics, mend choir robes, collect clothing for the needy, assist with children's choirs, and win ribbons in the church's annual art show.

Tithes and Gifts

Our elderly run the financial gamut from welfare to

riches. Many a tithe from baby-sitting is dropped proudly into the offering plate, like the widow's mite. Pensioners lay aside the Lord's tenth when they receive their monthly checks. (They fed and clothed their families through the Depression and know how to economize.) They tithe interest from savings. Retirees who have no family or whose children are financially independent name the church as beneficiary to bequests and life insurance policies.

Selling homes to move into apartments within walking distance of the church is a common practice among the elderly who are harrassed by yard work and increased taxes, and who are forced to give up driving. Some sign over their ownership of cars and trucks to the church. Many donate furniture, appliances and musical instruments.

Capital from sales of homes can be turned over to the church to provide the donor with a lifetime income from interest. The right to revoke all or part of the proceeds in case of emergency may be reserved. Some have deeded their homes to the church with the stipulation they be allowed to occupy them the remainder of their days. A newlywed senior adult couple donated $1500 toward the Youth Center. They reasoned that grandchildren of both families would derive benefits.

Unimproved properties have also been donated. Such as a parcel of beach acreage that increased in value, and its sale provided facilities for the church's retreat and conference campsite.

Retirees need to assess their resources, prepare long-range budgets including tithes and gifts, take advantage of income tax deductions which encourage philanthropy, and judiciously revise out-of-date wills. Matthew 6:20 tells us the safest place for us to lay up our treasures.

When the church's sanctuary was completed in 1965, a brochure listing needed furnishings was circulated. "Sacrificial giving will be necessary," Dr. Fickett told us. Ashamed of the tithe I had given from my retirement pension as compared with the unspeakable benefits I had derived, I took inventory. I had $1000 in a savings account bequeathed to the church I belong to at the time of my death. Why not withdraw that? Since I had dedicated it, I would never touch it for any other use.

A list of parts for the custom-built pipe organ filled three pages of the brochure. My $1000 would just about pay for the Viole de Gambe pipes (or "stop") on the

34

swell organ, or the Bourdon stop on the great organ. Every time I hear the set I chose I feel a sort of affinity for them. My gift was bread cast upon waters (Eccles. 11:1).

I was asked to fill a vacancy on the church school faculty. I taught long enough to replace the $1000, pay for a tour of the Holy Land and qualify for Social Security and Medicare.

Then one Sunday Dr. Fickett preached on Malachi 3:10: "Bring ye all the tithes into the storehouse . . . and prove me now herewith, saith the Lord of hosts, if I will not open you the windows of heaven, and pour you out a blessing, that there shall not be room enough to receive it." I was fully enjoying the Lord's blessings, and the Bible says it is more blessed to give than to receive. *All* the tithes? Now I have *two* sets of pipes to listen for. This keeps my mind from wandering during the offertory.

These examples of gifts are characteristic of older persons whose hearts are stayed on Christ and His church. A program for senior adults need not be a financial burden to a church who opens its doors and its heart to persons in special need of Christian fellowship, assurance, and the joy of serving to the end of their days. Dr. Fickett estimates that the Jolly Sixties contribute at least 100,000 hours of volunteer service annually to the church.

The church employs retired church members full or part-time for ministerial, clerical, maintenance, and custodial services.

A 198-unit, 12-story retirement apartment building, completed in spring 1974, opened with a waiting list of 300. Van Nuys Baptist Towers is a low-rental facility requiring neither an accommodation investment nor exorbitant entry fee. Tenancy is restricted to persons over sixty-two, but not to members of the church or the Jolly Sixties.

The building is situated sixty feet from the street, with landscaping, walkways, patios, parking, and outdoor recreation facilities. Individual air-conditioning and heating, solar glass windows, hand grips, and a twenty-four-hour instant communication system are some of the features which assure comfort and convenience. Tenants are required to eat at least one nourishing and balanced meal daily in the dining room to combat the "tea-and-toast syndrome" to which many elderly have fallen prey, causing mental and physical illness and degeneration. There are lounges, recreation and hobby rooms, and laundry facilities. Residents surrounded by friendly neighbors may choose companionship or solitude. They are free to travel, have a wealth of hobbies and services from which to choose, and are not burdensome to young relatives.

Footnotes

1. Paul W. Brauer, "The Art of Retirement," *Lutheran Witness* (Official periodical of the Lutheran Church, Missouri Synod, June, 1968).

PRAISE THE LORD WITH SONGS AND INSTRUMENTS

One evening when Dr. John Gustafson, minister of music at the church, sang for a Jolly Sixties social, he visualized his audience as a potential singing unit. Older voices, if well blended and trained, could glorify God and express joy and reverence. Has-been choristers could be restored to action. Non-churched music lovers might be motivated to attend church services where they would hear the gospel message. Why not give it a try? The Jollies caught the vibration. Eighty signed up, and within a few months took part in an all-church choir festival.

Singing Choir

After the sanctuary was completed, church membership increased at a phenomenal rate. Church ministry showed prospects of burgeoning into leadership of some thirty-five choirs ranging from cherubs to senior adults, plus chorales and ensembles, a day-school glee club, an orchestra, and several handbell choirs. A host of assistant directors had to be enlisted and trained. A member of the Christianaires ("Amen") choir, Elmer Ahl, volunteered to take on the Jolly Sixties choir.

The Jollies started with the hymnal for voice blending

nd to establish the sound of four-part harmony. But
at dated them and cramped their style. Now they are
nging spirituals, mod specialities, standard anthems in
om two to four parts, and contemporary arrangements
f hymns and gospel songs. Some of their selections
re enhanced by trumpet, melodica, or vibraharp obbli-
atos or by antiphonal singing of a trio, quartet, or solo
oice. They are scheduled to sing for several worship
ervices throughout the year and to fill in when other
hoirs are away on tour.

Instrumental Groups

A handbell choir of Jollies was organized but discon-
nued because the larger bells are too heavy for ringers
ith weak hearts or arthritis to lift and manipulate.

Harmonicas are closely related to some of the Old
estament instruments which were wholly acceptable
o God for worship. Juniors, scouts, campers, carolers,
obbyists, loners, professional musicians, and people of
ll ages with or without a music background can praise
iod with this pocket gadget.

The first harmonica class was offered to the Jolly
ixties in 1964. Fifty enrolled. Younger adults and two
ssociate ministers learned along with the oldsters. Ex-
erienced players encouraged and aided beginners.
Newcomers kept joining up. I can say with the Psalmist,
Unless the Lord had been my help (by drawing me
nto the Jolly Sixties), my soul had almost dwelt in
ilence" (Ps. 94:17).

Some in the class had dreamed of playing a musical instrument all of their lives. Some had sold their piano when the children left home and now hungered for a creative outlet. Others sought a hobby or planned to organize a youth group. A few needed breathing exercises recommended by their physicians. A few lonely persons just longed to belong. And so the old school teacher was back in the harness. A harness with bells and silver trappings. I made new friends from all walks of life.

As among the string, woodwind, brass and percussion families, there is a variety of harmonica models. We started with the C-tuned diatonic "Marine Band" model. Lacking a suitable repertoire, I transposed uncopyrighted hymns and gospel songs to the key of C and ran off copies on a duplicating machine. Playing everything in one key became monotonous and was inappropriate for many songs, so we bought G-tuned instruments. Eventually, we graduated to chromatic models on which we could sound sharps and flats by pressing in a lever. These made available to us most any selection within our technical ability.

First Lesson

There is a right and a wrong way to do almost anything, and harmonica playing is no exception. "To play tunes with clear single tones on a harmonica, we press the tongue firmly against the mouthpiece," I explained at our first lesson. "Place the instrument between th

40

lips and blow around the right side of the tongue like this." I demonstrated with some single tones, then with the scale.

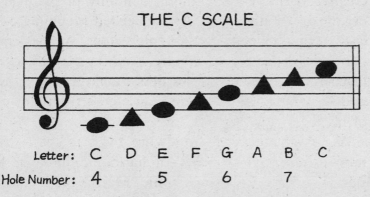

THE C SCALE

Letter: C D E F G A B C
Hole Number: 4 5 6 7

(I use triangular notes to indicate drawing or inhaling.)

I walked around the room aiding individuals. One woman resisted me. "You don't need to show *me* how to play this thing," she blustered. "I belong to a family of musicians."

"I learned to play mine upside down with numbers on the bottom," another pupil told me. "Do I have to learn all over again?" After hearing her play, I assured her it wasn't necessary.

While I was giving individual guidance, a man sitting next to my desk who said he just came to listen, picked up my instrument and played a lively march. Everyone stopped to listen and applauded.

"By cracky!" he exclaimed. "I haven't had a harp in my mouth for forty years. I could play as good as I used to if my upper plate didn't keep dropping down."

Applause, laughter, recommendations of adhesives,

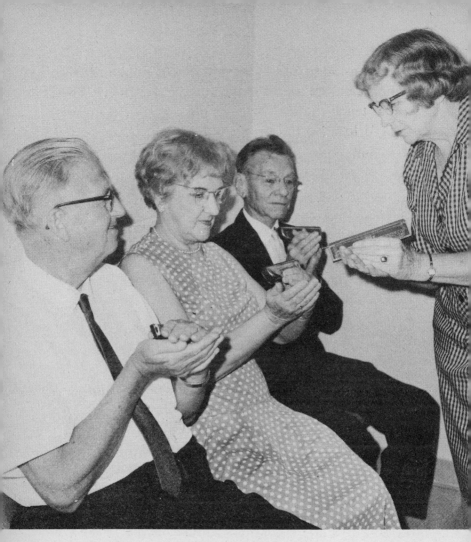

calls for encore. He complied with, "Oh! Susanna."

"'Oh! Susanna' is on page 9 in your book. Ben started by blowing into hole 4," I told the class. "Shall we try it?"

While they were opening their books, Ben countered, "I can't read notes. I learned to play by hole numbers."

I would as soon use a toothbrush secondhanded as a harmonica, so I told Ben he might keep the harp if he would teach the class how to play by hole numbers. He looked lost. So did my harmonica.

We scanned the score in the book as one would a road map, then they accompanied me as I played their first piece on the piano. Big thrill!

One man had his harmonica at his lips but hadn't opened his book. "I cain't read notes," he drawled.

"None of us could if we didn't look at them," I kidded him. "It's simple. When notes go up on the music staff, slide your harmonica to the left to play higher reeds. Draw in your breath for triangle notes and blow for the round ones."

We watched his perception open like a rose. "You mean you suck on the triangles and blow the bubbles?"

"Exactly!" I agreed. "Who says you can't read music?"

I had detected a professional tone quality emanating from the back of the room, and a reserved gentleman identified himself at this point. "I came to your class out of curiosity, to find out how the harmonica can be played by notes," he told me. "I was one of the original Minevitch 'Rascals.' We played by hole numbers. Mind if I stick around to get the hang of it?"

Embarked into Service

By the time the class learned to produce single tones by tonguing and a pleasing tone quality by manipulating

43

their hands, we were being urged to take part in the visitation ministry and play for services at convalescent hospitals on Sunday afternoons.

For eight years the harmonica choir has traveled on the first Sunday afternoon of each month by church bus to a convalescent hospital. Rev. Dale Scott, in charge of Special Services, gives the sermonette, Scripture reading and prayer, and drives the bus. Other "Jollies" accompany the harmonica choir. They wheel patients into the activity room and sing the gospel songs which we play on our harmonicas. Some minister to the bedfast during our 30- to 40-minute service. On the third Sunday, we accompany Dave and members of the singing choir to another rest home to play special numbers.

Our harmonica choir has been an outreach into the community, entertaining at local chapters of national clubs for the blind, grandmothers, indoor sports for handicapped and for veterans, Grange, Eastern Star and conventions as well as for church functions. On monthly bus outings we take our harmonicas along and lead in group singing.

An humble service? Yes! My adoption of the little mouth organ for Christian service reminds me of Victor Herbert. He took up the piccolo to fill a need for a program at the university where he was studying medicine. When he broke the news to his mother that he had decided to give up medicine to be a musician, she replied, "Do as you like, son. But why not pick on something your size?"

"Like what?" Victor asked.

"Look in the mirror. A cello. What else?" He took her advice.

If the harmonica is my size—or rather, if I am the size of the harmonica, I praise the Lord for my "gift of tongues." It keeps me humble.

Special Talents

We sometimes use an Autoharp for accompaniment. This glorified zither is related to the Old Testament psaltery, both comprised of a set of strings mounted on a resonating soundbox with no neck. A person too short-winded to play a harmonica can derive pleasure and make a valuable contribution by playing the Autoharp. An instruction book accompanies the instrument. It is a self-taught instrument. The durable steel strings hold pitch well, but it must be tuned to the harmonica reeds. There is no upkeep expense except for soft ukulele picks. I have used my Autoharp thirty-five years without having to replace a string. It provides a more delicate background for harmonicas than a piano, but its harmony is limited; so we were glad when a guitarist joined our choir.

When Dixie enrolled in my harmonica class, she had just pulled through a lengthy convalescence from a stroke and was seeking mental and spiritual therapy through music and Christian fellowship. She progressed faster than anyone else in my beginners' class and qualified for membership in the performing choir within a few weeks. About that time her daughter gave her a

guitar. We didn't discourage her harmonica playing, but put more pressure on chord strumming. We really needed that guitar. In no time Dixie memorized the most commonly used chords and continued to pick up the rarer sounds and beats. She inherited an Appalachian-style dulcimer made by her grandfather during Civil War days and delights audiences by plucking out tunes on one string while the other two give out a drone bass similar to bagpipes. Her most valued service to the group, however, is accompanying them on her guitar.

Harold, a former vaudeville trouper, was attracted to

46

the church through the harmonica class. He learned to play a chromatic with a beautiful tone quality, accepted Christ as his Saviour and Lord, joined the church, and dedicated his life to service. Harold's hobby was making and playing one-string fiddles. Whether he played "Mansion Over the Hilltop," "Blue Hawaii," or "Bali Hai," his exact pitch and soulful vibrato amazed and thrilled all who heard him. Wherever the harmonica choir entertained, he was a popular featured artist.

In his garage workshop Harold made twenty-five instruments which he presented to anyone who wished to learn to play, and gave them class lessons. No one succeeded in emulating Harold's mastery of the one-string fiddle, but everyone took pleasure in scraping and sawing through the evening, and his patience measured up to Job's.

Harold's rare art, his showmanship, refinement, immaculate grooming, thoughtfulness and delightful personality made him a favorite companion, entertainer, and member of the Jolly Sixties. A sadness fell over everyone when his frail body succumbed to pneumonia.

Harold's star pupil, Mabel, was another natural musician attracted to the church through the harmonica. One day she brought a new instrument to harmonica rehearsal—a reed instrument with a keyboard just over a two-octave compass, played with the mouth. Intrigued, several of us bought these melodica pianos and explored them together. We discovered that they take less breath than harmonicas. We didn't have to blow or draw. Just place the mouthpiece against the lower lip, position the tongue for "too," breathe into it, and out comes the music. Holding it is no problem, for it weighs about one pound. Its keys are smaller than piano keys and respond to a light touch. Double stops and triads can be played on a melodica, but take more breath, so we divided up for harmony. We found arrangements for ladies' trios suitable, and I made three- to six-part arrangements of spirituals, classics, and folk and patriotic selections. We play in all keys, unaccompanied.

Doctors encourage most people with pulmonary weakness to remain active and to do breathing exercises, unless they have an infection. Our players with asthma or heart trouble took a breath whenever they needed one, but practice increased control. Patients under a doctor's care should consult their physicians before investing in any wind instrument.

Mabel's husband, Clark, added variety to our repertoire with his accordion. He was a good harmonica player and possessed a lyric tenor voice, rare among men in the sixties. Both the instrumental and the singing organizations suffered when their failing health removed this couple from action.

As a school teacher, it was routine to me to train and part with pupils periodically. However, with older people, when parting is final, the tug on heart strings is grievous. Dropouts are not flunk-outs, but fade-outs.

The first step in combining the vocal and instrumental choirs was taken to furnish music for Saturday night religious services at the Union Rescue Mission on Skid Row in Los Angeles. Dave and Elmer transported members of the two choirs there on church buses three or four times a year. Dave preached the sermons, and Elmer and I directed anthems and instrumental gospel music.

On one of these trips, loyalty beyond the call of duty was demonstrated by a member of both choirs. Cecile had not felt well that day, but dutifully boarded one of the buses on the church lot. She lined up in front of the pulpit with the harmonica group and played alto, as usual, on our first package. Minutes later, when the choir was called upon to sing, she was unable to stand

49

up. After several attempts, she settled back in her seat and sang a true alto on the anthems. When we started to leave at close of the service, she slumped to the floor. Dave took her to the bus in a wheel chair, and from the church lot to a hospital. Cecile, in her eighties, had suffered a stroke from which she never fully recovered.

Praised for her faithfulness, Cecile said she was thankful she was not at home alone where she might have lain on the floor for days before being discovered. Cecile felt secure in the company of God's people.

Show and Tell

News got around southern California about the Jolly Sixties program, and inquiries came in from other churches wanting to initiate such a ministry. Would Dave come some Sunday and tell the congregation and staff how to go about it?

Dave thought, like most educators do, that it would be more effective to *show* and tell. He proposed bringing the choirs along and taking over an evening service. They bought that! Dave started preparing sermons and both music directors scheduled extra rehearsals.

Bus trips to Long Beach, Santa Ana, Whittier, Oxnard and other cities meant starting out in the afternoon with three busloads of musicians and paraphernalia, planning the agenda with staffs of host churches, seating ninety singers according to voice parts in spaces intended for twenty to forty, placing instrumentalists where they could move out to play, finding a spot to line them up, setting up sound equipment, and rehearsing the knottiest cacophonies. All of this prior to a meal for the "5000" provided by gracious ladies of the host church.

Limited rest-room facilities delayed action, since harmonica players clean their teeth before playing their instruments. Instrumentalists who couldn't hear instructions squeezed into far corners. Music stands got knocked over. The vibraharp bugged the sound system. Tongues of the thirsty cleaved to roofs of mouths. Stuffy air and hot robes converted music sheets to fans. Someone had a coughing spell during prayer.

The first few times we were out, I'm afraid we showed how *not* to do it! But once we established a routine, anticipated and adjusted to new situations and accepted it all as a challenge, we relaxed and enjoyed the trips.

After church was over there were exchanges of felicitations and handshaking, removal of robes, gathering of wraps and trappings, loading buses, the long ride back to church, returning robes to choir rooms and hanging them on proper racks, then trudging or driving home, only to lie awake until dawn, racked by tunes that wouldn't turn off.

In spite of fatigue, we were always ready to go the next time. Rocking chairs and slippers have not lured these servants of God, some in their eighties. "The way of the Lord is strength to the upright" (Prov. 10:29). King David was plagued with insomnia, too, and sang songs in the night. He advised communing with your own heart upon your bed and being still (Ps. 4:4). And

51

Elihu spoke of songs in the night to Job (Job 35:10). "A little sleep, a little slumber, a little folding of the hands" (Prov. 6:10), and Wednesday finds choir members in their places for 6:00 P.M. rehearsal, followed by prayer meeting and Bible study in the sanctuary.

Music Is Therapeutic

Response to music is innate, from lullaby days to final benediction. Therapeutic benefits have been known since the days of King Saul. Three million adults take up musical instruments every year. The simpler ones which are ready-tuned, inexpensive, lightweight, portable, reasonably durable, easy to manipulate, and which demand a minimum of physical effort can satisfy the needs of most older people for self-expression, fellowship, and for worship. Americans purchase 2,000,000 harmonicas every year. How many of them are used to glorify God?

At Convalescent Hospitals

I believe our harmonica choir's most effective function is our ministry at convalescent hospitals. The soft reeds do not drown out words of songs nor startle sensitive ears. We have learned to love the patients, and they look forward to our coming. Do you think such places are boring? Come and see!

At one hospital an attractive heart patient meets us at the door. A bright-eyed nonagenarian sets up chairs

and passes out song books. A minister, muted and crippled by a stroke, expresses warmth by kissing our hands. A Christian daughter visits her mother to share the service with her. A devoted husband for sixty years, his curly hair neatly parted in the middle, brings his "bride" in her wheelchair and holds her hand.

An old man sits with head back, eyes closed, breathing heavily with mouth open until we start our opening number. He straightens up, opens his eyes, smiles, and exclaims, "A harmonikey!" A withdrawn neurotic hugs a doll to her breast through the entire service. A malcontent rolls his chair back and forth, bumping into others whose responses range from tolerance to retaliation.

A slender, barefoot lady with flowing white hair listens intently to the music, rises to her feet, and dances in perfect rhythm. She is delicate and graceful and, like Moses' sister Miriam, sways her body and interprets the words of the song with her agile hands, arms, and lithe form. Someone leads her gently back to her chair. Throughout the singing she rises as the spirit moves her.

A chain smoker sits at a table lighting one cigarette with the butt of the last one unless the chain is interrupted by a coughing spell, in which case she sips cold coffee, strikes a match under the table, and starts afresh. The lap of her flimsy gown is pocked with burn holes. What a pity she didn't break the habit while she possessed the acuity! (In the National Fire Protection Association's latest annual report there were 16,600 fires in hospitals and homes for the aged. In one convalescent hospital thirty-one elderly persons perished.)

A blind woman with a strong voice throws up her arms and shouts praises to the Lord during the message. A nurse is paged over the public address system and a sour-faced woman yells, "Aw, shut up!"

One Sunday afternoon no speaker was available. To fill in, I selected a psalm and asked one of the men in our group to lead in prayer at the close of my talk. When Lou started praying, a woman took out her rosary. Most of her prayer was inaudible, but "Hail, Mary!" always seemed to be cued in when Lou reached the end of sentences.

Our closing song was "He Lives!" Perhaps I was more daring than usual that day because I was in full charge. I forgot my singing days were over and led out with gusto as I strummed my Autoharp, while others played their harmonicas.

A pretty patient in a ruffly blue negligee sitting in a wheelchair close by reached over and touched my hand when we finished the song. "Your voice is beautiful," she said.

I started to laugh it off, but the earnest expression on her face stopped me. I knew it wasn't my voice which touched her. The beauty she sensed was the spirit-to-spirit message of the song. She shared with me the risen Saviour who lived in both of our hearts. I hugged her and asked if she had a favorite song she would like sung before we left.

"Could we sing 'In the Sweet By and By'?" she asked.

I strummed a chord and she blended her quavering voice with the others.

"There's a land that is fairer than day,
   And by faith we can see it afar;
   For the Father waits over the way
   To prepare us a dwelling-place there."

My concept of beauty changed then and there. She was one of God's beautiful singers. The beauty was not from her vocal cords, but from the outpouring of her spirit in song. My eyes filled with tears, and I hurried out of the room. The song took me back to the evening

I spent with my dying grandmother when I was sixteen.

In those days, a paralytic stroke was the last strike. There were no rest homes or convalescent hospitals. Drugs did not destroy the beauty and pathos of a loved one's departure to glory. Grandma lay on her bed through the hot summer, her left side completely paralyzed. I often relieved the nurse in the evening and sat beside grandma's bed.

That night, she started singing, "In the Sweet By and By." She gasped for breath between trembling phrases, and I blended my voice with hers. While we were singing the chorus, she started tugging at her wedding ring. I thought it might feel tight and helped her to remove it.

She handed it to me. "Do you want me to have your ring, grandma?" I asked. She nodded her head.

I kissed her hand and put the ring on my finger. "Thank you, grandma!" I choked back the sobs. "I shall keep it forever."

She closed her drowsy eyes as though she were tired.

We were alone, and I was uneasy. The room was so still. Not a sound but the grandfather's clock across the hall keeping pace with her labored breathing. I took her cold hand in mine. "Grandma!" I tried to arouse her. "Sometime we'll sing that song together again."

She opened her eyes. The right corner of her mouth curled up into a faint smile. She nodded her head, closed her eyes again, and she was gone.

Prior to the Social Security Act of 1937, senior adults were not dubbed "senior citizens" and dumped into one stew pot. The term discounts the personal, cultural and spiritual qualities of this diffuse segment of society which has crashed the leisure class, formerly monopolized by the wealthy. Growing discontent with the label led to changing "Senior Citizens Month" to "Older Americans Month" in May, 1974.

People in the upper age bracket appreciate their citizenship and the many services rendered to them. They rank highest in casting their ballots in national elections. Yet citizenship simply designates a voter who owes allegiance to the government and is entitled to its protection.

Look closer, and you will see that no two are cut from the same pattern. Some 8,000 genes differentiate each person from all others, from the start. The more years we spend in diversified environments, pursuits, vocations, training, contacts, and experience, the more individualized we become. Also, living alone accentuates personality traits; for, when we are alone, we are completely ourselves.

Each of our 21 million adults, sixty-five years and over, is a separate book. Some you want to read from cover to cover and keep in a prominent place. Some you might peruse reluctantly like an assigned textbook for a required course of study. Some can be fathomed only one page at a time. There are psalmists who fluctuate from despair to composure to rapture, like King David; Solomons whose wisdom falls upon ears that hear not; Jeremiahs whose lamentations could impede the helter-skelter into Babylonian captivity; musicians whose harps have been hung on trees; and actors maintaining their stance before the footlights.

Are some boring because they live in the past? They have had a great deal of that, and their present may be a vacuum. Is their conversation a monologue of complaints? Urge them to seek medical advice if their complaints seem valid. Help them to escape from self-pity by cultivating other interests if they seem imagined.

I know a woman who had a nervous breakdown thirty years ago and is still enjoying poor health. I know another who came to California dying of cancer. Prayer and participating in activities of the church and the Jolly

Sixties is believed responsible for lengthening her life three years beyond the doctor's prediction.

A lonely person needs someone who will listen and uplift. He can be spiritually hungry without realizing the cause of his depression, his querulousness, his guilt complex or his poor self-image. Self-pity and loneliness can cause mental illness. E. O. Excell expressed the basic need for averting loneliness in one of his songs, "A Little Bit of Love":

"Do you know the world is dying
   For a little bit of love?
Everywhere we hear the sighing
   For a little bit of love.
For a love that rights a wrong,
   Fills the heart with hope and song;
They have waited, oh, so long,
   For a little bit of love."

The following poem, addressed to her son, was found in a mother's scrapbook after her death:

"Sitting alone by the window,
Watching the moonlit street,
Bending my head to listen
For the well-known sound of your feet,
I have been watching, darling,
Waiting and watching in vain
For the well-known sound of your footsteps
I long to hear again.

"All by myself I think of you,
Think of things we used to do,
Think of things we used to say,
Think of each golden yesterday.
Sometimes I sigh, sometimes I cry,
But keep each golden moment
All to myself."

—Elaine Vetter

The Happy People

Superlative grace is needed by persons who have passed through stress and strain, pain and suffering, loss of loved ones, neglect and inertia, to enable them to face an indefinite era of more of the same. Our church is preeminent in providing spiritual strength, opportunity for fellowship and service, study of God's Word in depth, prayer for one another, the joy of being accepted, and the ability to accept one's self. Dr. Fickett's favorite name for the Jolly Sixties is "the happy people."

A sweet Christian spirit prevails notably among the older members. This was strikingly demonstrated to me one cold Wednesday night. Rain was falling in torrents, and streets were flooded above curbs when mid-week Bible study was dismissed. I had taught school all day, conducted two rehearsals, and had to be back to teach in the morning. Driving home meant bucking drenched intersections and low visibility, riding brakes, and the chance of skidding and losing control.

Instead, I found myself across the street from the

church, snug and cozy amidst colonial maple furniture, hook rugs and samplers, facing a stranger who was my hostess.

"I'm glad I overheard you asking about a motel," she was saying pleasantly. "There was no need of you driving miles across the Valley or going to a motel. Make yourself at home while I fix some hot tea."

Minnie was tall and slender, with white hair pinned back in a knot. She appeared to be in her upper seventies. By the time I shared the hot breakfast she prepared the next morning, I had learned that she was secretary of her Sunday School class and White Cross chairman for her missionary circle. She spent two days a week visiting new church members and the sick. She told me of a mother, whose child had been killed by a hit-and-run driver, whom she had tried to console, about a newly converted young couple she was guiding in Bible study, and the blind man she read to every Tuesday. Friday mornings found her at Bible study and the church-bulletin preparation project. Though her apartment was within a few steps of the church, she drove her car to transport non-drivers to and from services. And she dropped some cookies in my lunch sack, that were left over from a batch she had baked for an orphanage.

Minnie joined my harmonica class and was faithful in her many branches of service up to her sudden death. Her memorial service was held in the main sanctuary in order to accommodate the hundreds who came to pay her tribute.

I look forward to visiting Minnie in her lovely mansion

over the hilltop, with which I am sure the Lord has rewarded her. When I was a stranger, she took me in.

Mabel and Herman

Our oldest Jolly Sixty has been a widow since 1914. Mabel was a charter member in the singing and harmonica choirs and took to the harmonica readily when she was eighty-seven. On bus trips she would play with others by the hour. We gave her a chromatic model for her ninetieth birthday. She seldom missed a rehearsal or a performance until she was hospitalized with a stroke just before she was ninety-five. She expressed regret to me that her doctor told her she would have to slow down and drop out of music.

A few years ago she and her daughter (with whom she lives) flew to Iowa in mid-winter for an extended visit. While we at home were praying that she wouldn't slip on ice and break her hip, she was describing the beauty of the scenery in verse:

"Did you ever stand in winter
  Just inside the window sill?
See the little flakes of whiteness
  Make great mounds out on the hill?

"Did you ever once consider
  How these things all came to be?
From whence these scenes of beauty
  That are here for you and me?

"It was a hand of beauty,
    It was a hand of love,
It was the hand of our heavenly Father
    From His home high up above."
                    —Mabel Baldwin

The poet laureate of our organization, in his nineties, is a writer of epic, doggerel, paraphrase, and whimsy verse. Ninety-one-year-old Herman can spontaneously improvise on most any subject for any occasion, often with tongue in cheek. Though cataracts have been removed from both eyes, he reads a great deal and memorizes poetry. Six feet tall, he is as straight as a ponderosa pine.

Living alone in his own home, Herman keeps house, cooks, washes and irons his clothes, cultivates hybrid roses, and takes care of his yard. He mows the lawn for a neighbor who isn't able to do such strenuous work! For a number of years, his special church project has been serving the blind in various ways. He also enjoys social functions of a civic club for "senior citizens."

When Herman heard that Dr. Fickett was to attend a Jolly Sixties social one night, he composed and read the following tribute:

THE PASTOR

"When the game seems up and time runs out
    With threat of dire disaster,
Who's in there pitching his heart out?
    You've guessed it! It's the pastor.

"Or when we need a friend the most,
Who gets there any faster?
We always find him at his post—
Your friend and mine, the pastor.

"When I am stricken unto death
And pale as alabaster,
I'll whisper with my latest breath,
'God bless you, my good pastor.'

"Some day a messenger of love
Will beckon to the pastor
And say to him, 'Come up above.
Sit here beside the Master.' "

—Herman Guntner

Retired to Serve

Geriatricians are dispensing advice by the ton to prospective retirees on how to use their anticipated leisure time. Yet these specialists don't seem to give a thought to the Lord's plans for the rest of our lives. Sometimes He moves in a mysterious way and "the best laid plans of mice and men" are in vain. He is the One who granted us these bonus years. Surely He has purpose in all that He does! Why not seek His guidance?

Take Chuck Akley for example. Chuck was a group leader in the Processing Department of the Bendix Corporation for twenty-four years. His Christian service was working with children. Chuck began by teaching a junior

64

Sunday School class. From teaching he stepped to director to superintendent to coordinator. In the latter capacity he headed seven junior departments with as many superintendents and associate superintendents, sixty teachers, a bevy of secretaries, pianists, and song leaders. Chuck held meetings for outreach leaders and recruited and trained teachers and a staff for summer and winter camps. He personally counseled children in accepting Christ as their Saviour.

Then came the blow. A detached retina! Six operations! During the last one, the eye hemorrhaged and sight was gone. Now a cataract is developing on the other eye. His doctor does not recommend surgery on that eye for fear it might rupture and cause total blindness. Chuck has walking vision and uses strong magnifying glasses for other purposes. He took disability retirement from Bendix and retired as administrator in the Sunday School.

Recently a cataract started clouding my right eye and I panicked. Wakeful nights drew me to Psalm 77—excellent for anyone engulfed in self-pity. Humbly the Psalmist concurs; "This is my infirmity: but I will remember . . . thy wonders of old" (Ps. 77:10,11). Isaiah reminded me that God will keep me in perfect *peace* when my mind is stayed on Him (Isa. 26:3). Who am I that I should expect my *anatomy* to be kept perfect, too? After all, my left eye is unblemished. Cataracts develop slowly and 95 percent of them are successfully removed by surgery. With Chuck's example and God's precious Word brimming with comfort and cheer, my attitude loomed as ridiculous as when I lost my singing voice.

Did Chuck give up and crawl into a hole? No way! He prayed to be guided where he could serve the Lord effectively. And where did God lead this man with impaired eyesight? Into the church library where he works as a volunteer four afternoons a week. He loves it! He knows and loves the school children who browse there and withdraw books. He has learned the Dewey Decimal System and can help readers locate any of the 8000 books, the magazines, records, cassette tapes, Braille material, and reference books on the shelves.

Chuck loved music but never played an instrument until he took up the harmonica. He memorizes music readily, has a good ear, and plays on a professional level. He is in demand as soloist, in a trio, and with the harmonica choir.

And that is not all! His administrative expertise was so greatly needed, he is back as interim director of the fifth and sixth grade Sunday School department. Dr. Fickett describes Chuck as "one of the greatest and most effective junior workers the Holy Spirit ever brought to a church."

God also worked in a mysterious way with a machinist from Ohio who served the Lord there as a part-time ordained minister. When Fred Cooper moved his family to the San Fernando Valley he noted that 18 percent of the population were of Spanish-American heritage. He became interested in these people, their language, and their spiritual needs. His background consisted of only two years of Spanish in high school some forty-five years ago. Fred learned the language, built up a fluent biblical vocabulary, and established rapport with the people by rubbing elbows with them, studying textbooks, and attending a Spanish-speaking Baptist church for seven years. He started a Sunday School class for non-English-speaking Chicanos, using Bibles, hymnals, and quarterlies in Spanish. The class also became beneficial for church members wishing to brush up on their Spanish.

Rev. Cooper translates biblical texts and teaching materials into Spanish, and periodically crosses the border to conduct evangelical crusades in Mexican villages.

A Special Ministry

Another retiree chosen for special ministries is Randy Bramble, formerly employed at North American Rockwell. His wife, Edith, has been teaching mentally retarded children in a county school for ten years. You might think she would want to escape from what is regarded as a depressing climate, on weekends. But Edith loves the afflicted and deprived so much that she has infected her husband—and her daughter also—with her dedication and zeal.

The family volunteered to organize and teach a Sunday School class for young adult retardates. The church with the slogan, "A Church with a Vision," supported them. Some of the twenty who enrolled in their class

are transported to and from church by bus. Happily they vie to stand beside Randy when he sings for them, find pages in song books, memorize short Scripture passages, remember Bible stories from week to week, and give personal testimonies for Christ.

Because converts living in some boarding homes are discriminated against and denied the right to attend church by non-Christian superintendents, Edith has retired from teaching to become supervisor in a new Christian home for the mentally retarded.

Randy is a baritone recording artist of gospel songs and his musical talent is dedicated to the Lord. Another ministry has developed from his custom of singing for the unfortunate: the Brambles present, or engage others to provide, monthly programs for veterans, elderly, blind and crippled patients in half a dozen institutions.

Love Suffereth Long and Is Kind

The misfortunes of isolated, handicapped persons often tend to dominate their lives. When a church brings them together where the spirit of Christian love prevails and sets them in motion, they learn to understand, forbear, and accept one another as they are. Being accepted by others helps them adjust to their own limitations—even to joke about them!

A blind woman advised a friend who was losing her sight to keep her sense of humor so she could laugh at herself instead of withdrawing in embarrassment when she faced the wrong direction to pledge allegiance to the flag, sat in someone else's chair, or discovered at the end of an eventful day that she had spilled egg on her front at breakfast.

God has provided grace to bear our burdens and has admonished us to share others'. The Jolly Sixties organization is an experimental laboratory wherein His precepts are continually being tested and proven.

THE JOLLY ROAD TO ROMANCE

Recurrent association in social and service projects suggests romance. In the Jolly Sixties are men and women who share the same faith, seek the same spiritual leadership, and enjoy doing the same things. Rubbing shoulders with devoted couples who have been married fifty to sixty years stimulates nostalgia and can cause a sting of envy among those who have lost their lifetime companions. Is the Jolly Sixties organization a matrimonial bureau? If not, why not?

The first stumbling block is a matter of simple arithmetic. Among the 1500 currently on the roll there are 248 married couples, 906 lone women, and only 98 lone men. Statistically, more baby boys are born in the United States than girls, but the death rate right from the first few weeks is higher by 30 percent. Ultimately, women outnumber men by 79 percent. Explanations for this variance are numerous.

The female hormone estrogen is said to prolong life. Women's mortality in childbirth has been practically eliminated, and child delivery has established women's confidence in the medical profession. They go to their doctors when ill and for checkups. Men tend to regard this as unmasculine, though they are more susceptible to coronary and cardio-vascular diseases. They eat and drink in disregard to health factors and tend to worry more. In sports, the majority are sedentary spectators rather than active participants.

Women have already passed through the menopause, liberating them from periodic slavery to cycles, before retirement age. They have adjusted psychologically to their chicks flying the coop. The euphoria of "women's lib" is a reality. The greatest adjustment a wife has to make to retirement is having an idle man around the house.

The home has always been the woman's realm whether or not she holds an outside job, while a successful business or professional man forced to retire from a rewarding position loses status and identity. Being sent home like a naughty schoolboy gives him a feeling of guilt and defeat and deflates his ego, unless he has made plans for his new era.

The average life expectancy for women is six or seven years longer than for men. Since young men tend to marry girls about three years younger than themselves, widowhood of some eight to ten years would be the norm for the so-called "weaker sex." By the age of sixty-five, widows outnumber widowers four to one.

The situation is not a contemporary milieu. Widows are mentioned throughout the Bible. Jesus did not seem to regard the Sadducees' riddle about the woman who outlived seven husbands as unreasonable. (See Mark 12:18-23.)

In the upper age bracket death frequently stalks the marriage altar. Both members take that risk, but more often than not the woman remains to mourn—partly because men still tend to prefer younger partners. One couple in their seventies was happily married only two months when he died in his sleep. Another woman's fiance was rushed to the hospital with a fatal heart attack one week before their wedding date.

Stumbling Blocks to Romance

Couples may be influenced by their grown children who can be as vociferous in their objection as parents sometimes are about their children's marriages. Children can be every bit as meddlesome as those berated mothers-in-law we joke about.

Sometimes money is a stumbling block to romance. Suppose a widow is receiving her deceased husband's Social Security income, a percentage of his employee's pension, and a trust fund as long as she remains single. She falls in love with a man whose sole income is the minimum rate of Social Security. He will not ask her to forfeit her financial security by proposing marriage. So they just go steady.

In a first marriage when a couple is young, they can

establish a mutual living pattern. In a later marriage each has established his or her routine and customs. Adjustments must be made at every turn. One is a night owl, the other is up with the lark. One is punctual, the other can't be rushed. To one, money is a commodity to be used; the other is a pinch-penny. One counts dollars by the mile, the other is afraid to board a plane.

Taking a walk is a tug-of-war, for one saunters while the other strides or trots. One dotes on mementos and geegaws, the other hates clutter. One thrives on operas, concerts, clubs, entertainment. The other is a jealous, possessive introvert. Add to these dissimilarities habits of cleanliness and grooming, eccentricities, comparisons with the first (and always "perfect") spouse, the risk of eventually having an invalid to care for, and perhaps snoring. (Snoring? Don't laugh! According to the American Medical Association, snoring of at least 20,000,000 Americans breaks up friendships, campouts, and marriages.)

Marriage for companionship without deep affection may not be a happy solution for loneliness. The same is true for convenience marriages, when a man unschooled by his deceased wife in the arts of homemaking or a woman ungrounded in business affairs by her former husband marries solely to be taken care of. Such fortuitous marriages could be prevented if couples would foresee and forestall such an eventuality.

If the elderly were as hopelessly set in their ways as it appears, few "twilight marriages" would be happy. On the contrary, statistics show that late marriages have

increased 33 percent within a ten year period and that 95 percent are successful.

Today's furor of ponderous probing into the virility of older persons would surely have been idle prattle to Sarah and Abraham who both laughed about the pleasure of sex relationship almost 4000 years ago, at the ripe old ages of ninety-one and a hundred years. Laughter may be reaction to embarrassment, to the incredible, or to humor; but generally it is an expression of joy. And then came Isaac! (See Genesis 17 and 18.)

Success in Marriage

From couples for whom the Jolly Sixties organization has functioned as a matrimonial bureau I have gleaned the following recipes for success:

You have to love your mate more than yourself, have a strong desire to please, be willing to give more than you take, and not expect a reformation after the knot is tied. One should either cultivate a yen for the partner's special interests or be tolerant of them. Be willing to sacrifice privacy. Talk over *everything* in advance to really know each other. Try to establish a harmonious relationship with children on both sides. If either has property intended for members of the families other than the new spouse, have an attorney draw up a prenuptial financial contract, and up-date wills.

Have a pre-marriage counseling session with the minister who is to perform the wedding ceremony. Establish a family altar for daily prayer and Bible study.

Then, hand in hand, walk boldly and serenely together to the end of the rainbow.

Can old people change? adjust? adapt? They can if they want to!

WHO WANTS TO
GROW OLD?
AND HOW TO AVOID IT

The blessing or the threat of aging is largely a matter of attitude. Do we dread it? fear it? fight it? accept it? embrace it? or surrender to it? Actually, we start aging when we are born, and we travel a one-way street. Growing old is a synonym for progress, development and maturation. *Getting* old implies succumbing to a condition, like catching a disease. But they tell us there are no old-age diseases. It's just that our machinery shows wear from being on the road so long. The longer we journey, the more hazards we encounter.

Dora Johnson, in her upper eighties, refutes senility in her own charming style:

"You tell me I am getting old;
    I tell you that's not so!
The house I live in is worn out,
    And that, of course, I know.
It's been in use a long, long while,
    It's weathered many a gale;
I'm really not surprised you think
    It's getting somewhat frail.

"The color's changing on the roof,
    The windows getting dim,
The walls a bit transparent
    And looking rather thin.
The foundation's not so steady
    As once it used to be;
My 'house' is getting shaky
    But my 'house' isn't me!

"A few short years can't make me old—
    I feel I'm in my youth;
Eternity lies just ahead,
    A life of joy and truth.
I'm going to live forever, there!
    Life will go on—it's grand!
You tell me I am getting old?
    You just don't understand!

"The dweller in my little 'house'
    Is young and bright and gay—
Just starting on a life to last

Throughout eternal day.
You only see the outside,
    Which is all that most folks see;
You tell me I am getting old?
    You've mixed my 'house' with me!"[1]

We hear it said that we are as old as we feel—old as we look—old when we stop looking—old as our arteries. Victor Hugo regarded forty as the old age of youth and fifty the youth of old age. Oliver Wendell Holmes thought it more cheerful to be seventy years young than forty years old. Dr. Ethel Percy Andrus found age a victory, not a defeat; a privilege, not a punishment. When General Douglas MacArthur was seventy-five, he expressed his philosophy about youth and age thus, "Youth is not a time of life. It is a state of mind. You are as young as your faith, as old as your doubt; as young as your self-confidence, as old as your fears; as young as your hope, as old as your despair."

Life and Time

In our youth-oriented culture, old people are victims of the same conspiracy to engender self-pity as are other minorities: the Negro, the Indian, the Mexican, as well as the blind, deaf, alcoholic, dope addict and the criminal.

Yet each is the recipient of the world's most valuable commodities: life and time. They are a sacred trust. And who but oldsters have the most of both? By permitting us to grow old, our gracious Lord enables us to compensate for time we have wasted. Why do we mark time, pass time, spend time, waste time, and kill time instead of investing it? If the poet's desire, "Backward, turn backward, O time in your flight," could be realized, would we put it to better use? Methuselah lived 969 years. And for what contribution to humanity was his name perpetuated? He had a grandson named Noah! (See Gen. 5:25-29.)

There are people who view age with resignation and confuse it with senility. When one woman in her forties lost her husband, she moved in with her daughter's family, parked her rocking chair by the hearth, and folded her hands.

For some, the concept of retirement vacillates, as expressed humorously by one of our Jolly Sixties, Charles Malcolm Crocker:

"When I retire, I'm telling you
    A million things I've planned to do.
  It seems that I can hardly wait
    To check the time and keep that date.

"I'll weed the lawn and trim the hedge
    And pulverize the flower bed;
  I'll irrigate and fertilize
    Till every plant is giant size.

"And in the patio I'll check
    The easy chairs—Oh! What the heck!

I think right here I'll just recline
And wake up when it's time to dine."

You've seen the egoists who suffer torture to deny age. They give up reading by refusing to wear glasses; lose out on conversation by thumbing down a hearing aid; lean heavily upon companions, too "proud" to carry a cane. They feign ignorance about pre-World War I happenings and disdain association with the Geritol set. They'd rather swing with the swingers and rap with the teenyboppers. Are they really young at heart? Or are they seeing through a glass darkly?

It behooves self-respecting persons of all ages to keep up-to-date so far as is appropriate. Old people, like old barns, need renovating and touching up. Do those old men with hairy bowlegs you meet at the supermarket look young? Or the women with heavy makeup extending into the hairline and ending abruptly along the jawbone? What about those who wear short, tight skirts and neglect to practice sitting properly before a full-length mirror? No teen-ager would be as indiscreet. Trying to imitate youth does not make us youthful.

Far more venerable are those who embrace the latter years. Pearl Buck, working on three novels when she was seventy-nine, said she wouldn't want to be young again because she wouldn't want to lose all she had learned. It would be like failing to pass a grade.[2]

In an article on "Retirement Shock" in *Modern Maturity magazine,* Dr. Edward L. Bortz said; "When a person retires *from* life, life retires from *him.*"[3]

Ways to Avoid Aging

Yes, people can *avoid* growing old. They do every day. How? By neglecting to have periodic health check-ups; by ignoring symptoms of terminal diseases; by suicide; in major disasters. Half of us Americans are overweight, a contributory factor to several fatal diseases. Lives of alcoholics are shortened on an average of twelve years. Death from lung cancer is ten times what it was thirty years ago; from emphysema the increase in the past ten years is 1200 percent! Accidents took the lives of 117,000 last year. Improper or illegal use of guns destroys 21,000 annually in accidents, suicides, and murders. Thus modern man has contrived numerous means whereby he can avoid growing old. Yet Christ came that we might have life, and that we might have it abundantly.

Young at Heart

A better way is to stay young—at heart, that is! Not as an unknowing child, but with the poise, expertise and compassion we acquired while we were plunging pell-mell through the roaring '20s, terrible '30s, fearful '40s, frenzied '50s, and swinging '60s.

Pablo Picasso, still at his easel in his nineties, believed that a man who failed to render service according to his ability was not a man.

The hotel tycoon, Conrad Hilton, says in his autobiography that successful living consists of usefulness, contentment, and fulfillment of our particular talents; that each will fit into a divine pattern if and when he finds his niche.[4]

Dr. Charles LeRoy Lowman who founded the Orthopaedic Hospital in Los Angeles fifty years ago spent his ninety-fourth birthday on Christmas with Santa, distributing toys and showering affection in the children's wards. "The way you live and take care of yourself determines whether you are old at thirty-five or young at ninety," he told TV audiences.

Rev. Harold Cook writes from Brazil where he conducts weekly prayer meetings and preaches every Sunday in Portuguese at age ninety-six: "Nothing to do spells unhappiness and vegetation. For Christians, there is work to be done. I would rather die in the pulpit than in bed."

Dr. William Hinderliter was ordained as a minister when he was eighty-one. Tall, upright, with a sense of humor and a love for God and people, he was still serving on the staff at Angelus Temple in Los Angeles as visitation minister, at age 108 years. "Serve God and He will take care of you," he asserts.

Retirement Income

If growing old still lurks like a sword of Damocles over your head, consider the ever-increasing goodies waiting to fall into your lap when you arrive at that magic age.

One of the big concerns of prospective retirees is, "Will I be able to maintain my standard of living on my retirement income?" Actually there are as many elderly in the affluent economic bracket as in the low income. The news media's incessant spotlight on the latter has no doubt given you the dithers. Both singles and couples are living comfortably on pensions which amount to half of their former gross earnings. Those fat withholdings are ended. Less money is needed for clothes, transportation, lunches, dues, and keeping up with the Joneses. Thousands have found it economical and less work to reduce their living space; also to investigate locations where the cost of living is lower, and thus expand their horizons.

More than 90 percent of American retirees have pensions. Twenty-nine million elderly and disabled persons receive social security, 7000 of whom are 100 or more years old! Veterans' benefits were raised ten to twenty percent in 1974, and federal employees were granted automatic cost-of-living increases. The increase applies also to social security benefits starting January, 1975, and to some teachers' pensions. A 1974 pension reform bill guarantees retirement benefits to all workers covered by private pension plans.

Under the liberalized Keogh Act, savings and loan associations offer a pension savings plan for self-employed, whereby they can invest up to ten percent of their earned income per year. Both principal and interest are tax-free. Another savings plan enables workers not covered by employers to put aside up to 15 percent of their wages, tax-free.

The most opportune time for parents to invest in

savings which will provide supplementary income is after the children go on their own and the mortgage is paid off. I know a couple in their thirties who decided to save their dollar-a-day cigarette money. They figured that in thirty years their investment, not counting accumulated and compounded interest, would amount to $10,950. Six percent just on the principal would yield $54.75 a month. If they don't need it to live on or for emergencies, they plan to take a world cruise. A couple in their fifties have a $5000 savings account which will amount to over $9000 in ten years, at six percent compounded interest.

The Federal Government provides supplemental security income to 5.6 million needy which the home states supplement, plus medical assistance, in-home care and counseling.

To mollify a temporary money shortage or the initial shock of being discarded, you might like a part or full-time job. Consider Over 65, 40 plus, Upjohn's Homemakers, Inc., CLEAR (Continued Employment for the Retired, Inc.) or local opportunities. The Federal Government offers the Peace Corps, VISTA, Foster Parents, SCORE, ACE, and RSVP. Contact ACTION, Washington, D.C. 20525.

Twenty million more Americans between 55 and 64 years are retiring at the rate of 4000 per day. The wisdom of compulsory retirement at age 65 is being increasingly challenged for persons willing and able to work. Society is being robbed of their expertise and their contribution to the national economy. Military personnel can retire at the end of twenty years of service. Postal service employees can retire at age 50 with 20 years of service, and at any age after serving 25 years. Early retirees often enter a new field of action. In the same state city schools retire teachers at 65, county schools at 70. Changes may be in the offing, but 65 isn't so bad.

Special Privileges

Think of the double tax exemptions, retirement income credit, and tax-free social security or railroad retirement income the Internal Revenue Service has ready to hand you; the reduction or elimination of profit tax on sale of your property many states offer; tax and rent reductions on dwellings! You'll get reduced bus fares and entry fees to ball games, concerts and fairs. Golden Age passports will admit you free to all National Parks. You'll qualify for noncancelable health and auto insurance policies.

Housing, specially designed and constructed for old folk, covers a wide spectrum: urban hotels, boarding homes, apartment houses, condominiums, mobile homes, and retirement communities. Federally subsidized and insured housing programs for the elderly cover individual home loans, home improvement loans, housekeeping units, congregate housing, garden-type and high-rise developments, townhouse projects, and nursing homes.

Kind hearts and gentle people abet our desultoriness about marketing, cooking, and eating alone. For example, seven cafeterias in greater Los Angeles have been serving balanced meals, including dessert and beverage, to senior adults seven days a week for one dollar ever since 1969. A chain in Dade County, Florida, operates a similar service.

A national nutrition program operated by the federal government in cooperation with local authorities is providing noon meals five days a week to some 200,000 elderly, served in rural and urban centers. The cost is sixty or sixty-five cents, but persons on the poverty level may pay what they can or eat free. Meals are even being delivered to the housebound. Our music group entertained sixty or more diners at a local center one day, and found the meal tasty, adequate, and well balanced.

Some lodges and hotels—Sheraton, Rodeway, Marriott, Treadway, Howard Johnson and TraveLodge, for example—have granted older guests with ID cards reduced rates.

Recreation and park departments of cities and counties provide varied programs of social, cultural and educational activities for "senior citizens."

There are banks which do not charge for checking accounts. Theaters and fairs feature us on special days. Two hundred elderly persons were given watch dogs by the Los Angeles Department of Animal Regulation. More books are being published in large print. Amplified sound systems are being installed in more churches.

Universities and colleges are offering us courses tuition-free. Fairleigh Dickinson University at Madison, New Jersey, and North Hennepin State Junior College at Brooklyn Park, Minnesota, set the precedent. When oldsters by the score registered for everything from fly fishing to earning a degree (they even held rap sessions with the kids!) other schools followed suit. We may audit or enroll for credit.

For two dollars (annual dues) you can join hands with 5,000,000 retirees in the American Association of Retired Persons (AARP) and enjoy a bag of goodies, including a subscription to the magazine, *Modern Maturity*. AARP is sister organization to the National Retired Teachers Association. Both have chapters in hundreds of communities. A third division called Action for Independent Maturity (AIM) is geared to help persons between ages fifty and sixty-four prepare for those crowning years.

Experimental gerontology has reached stampede impetus. Medical researchers are probing into the effects of heredity, exercise, diet, mental activity, and attitudes on the timing of our destruction clocks, hoping to enable us to be self-sufficient right up to the countdown.

Now who doesn't want to grow old? You have survived infancy, childhood, school days, adolescence, family life, and long years of breadwinning. Father Time doesn't necessarily press a button and eject you, like a jack-in-the-box, into a dismal pasture to await the grim reaper. It's the *fear* of aging that is fatal to the fainthearted. "You are as young as your faith—as old as your fears."

In his report about a National Congress on the Quality of Life in the Later Years arranged by the American Medical Association in April 1974, the executive director of NRTA-AARP, Mr. Bernard E. Nash, stated, "We recognized that attitudes of individuals as they reach their later years are determined by previous patterns of living. If we have had experiences to enrich the mind and spirit during our youth and middle years, we will accept old age with good grace and find a new enrichment.... The self-renewing person never ends the development of his potentials."

"For age is opportunity no less
Than youth itself, though in another dress;
And as the evening twilight fades away
The sky is filled with stars, invisible by day."
                    —Henry Wadsworth Longfellow

Footnotes

1. Dora Johson, "You Tell Me I Am Getting Old," *Swedish Medical Center Journal,* Englewood, CO, (December 1965), p. 3.
2. Pearl Buck, "Essay on Life," *NRTA Journal,* Ojai, CA, (November-December, 1971), p. 52.
3. Edward L. Bortz, "Prescription for Retirement Shock," Dynamic Maturity, AARP, Ojai, CA, (November 1968), p. 52.
4. Conrad Hilton, *Be My Guest* (Prentice-Hall, Inc.: Englewood Cliffs, N.J., 1957), pp. 343-344.

Normally, life as a retiree falls into three stages. The first is the *get-up-and-go stage.* Your retirement notice is a declaration of independence. At last you can rekindle those dreams and ambitions your young heart had to discard when you became self-supporting, and bring about their realization. You have time to do what you've always wanted to do. You can go fishing, camping, globetrotting; curl up in an easy chair and read; chitchat over the back fence; tell off editors and newscasters you have been wanting to set straight on issues.

Now is the time to take an active part in your church program, lodge, club or society; give rein to your altruistic impulse to do unto others what needs to be done. We are pioneers setting a pattern and a pace for future generations by the manner in which we use our leisure time.

If you are too lethargic at first to do anything but throw the alarm clock out the window, stretch out and relax, do just that! Don't feel guilty. There are no rules on sick leave for you, no pay deductions, no stacks of back work piling up until you return to the grind. For you, the grinding mill has closed down. Once rested, doing nothing will be boring, unless that is all you want to do. In which case you will miss the first dynamic stage and skid into the second.

On the other hand, if you invested all you had in your career and anticipate facing a blank wall, then look the world in the face and dare to be honest enough to admit that there are more happenings going on than what was formerly your thing.

You are as precious in the sight of God as you always were. He has a plan for the rest of your life. Investigate! Explore! Adapt! Socialize! Exchange your mirror for a telescope. Let your real self-image emerge from that professional shell which may have isolated you from your family and friends. Don't destroy your true identity by wearing that mask after the ball is over. Let it fall with a hearty laugh and a characteristic gesture which will release the real you. Now is the beginning of the rest of your life. Retire *to* something and make the get-up-and-go era an adventure.

When Winston Churchill was sixty, he thought holding offices of state for twenty-four years had been enough. "I don't care whether I ever hold office again or not," he said. But England and the rest of the free world cared.

George Washington "retired" at the end of the Revolutionary War. What if his first retirement had been final?

Benjamin Franklin was a forceful member of the Constitutional Convention when he was eighty-one. Clara Barton was still engrossed full-time in Red Cross work when she was ninety.

You are not in their genius class, you say? Do you remember what Longfellow said about that in his "Psalm of Life?"

"Lives of great men all remind us
   We can make our lives sublime,
   And departing, leave behind us
   Footprints on the sands of time."

Scores of centenarians are actively engaged in projects they hope to complete.

Why Bother?

Eventually, you may gradually slither into the second stage of retirement—*the why-bother stage*—without realizing it. Or a serious illness or crippling accident may shift you abruptly into second gear. Even then, if you have the power and the will, you may overcome and shift back into high.

I know a teacher who had such a severe stroke a few months after she retired that she could neither walk, talk, read, nor recognize friends for two years. But she had a healthy body, clean living habits, and countless friends praying for her. When Gladys was able to leave the hospital, her husband and other members of the family did all in their power to encourage her and to restore her memory. Monte kept her in touch with former acquaintances, took her on trips where they had been before, browsed with her through photo albums and slides. She responded to this therapy and applied her mind zealously. A teacher with forty years of experience and winner of the Golden Apple for outstanding service, she even learned the multiplication tables all over again! Gladys is back with the get-up-and-goers. She and Monte have traveled all over the world.

Gus was a saint who glided from the first stage into his final home with the Lord. He was a big-boned, hardy farmer from South Dakota and a musician who played the violin, harmonica and melodica, and sang bass in the Jolly Sixties choir. He sold real estate, and he took care of an invalid wife for seven years. When left alone, he took offices in his Sunday School class and the Jolly Sixties organization, went out on church visitation twice a week, and performed innumerable services for his Lord. As he lay dying from a coronary occlusion, he led his hospital roommate and the man's wife to Christ.

In *the why-bother stage,* your exhilaration decelerates into a what's-the-use-of-running-when-there's-plenty-of-time-to-walk attitude. A medical checkup might reroute you back on the go-go, but it's too much bother if you have already yielded. What are some symptoms to watch for?

You'll be getting ready to attend a function you have always enjoyed when the thought comes to you that you don't *have* to go. The feeling of relief is decidedly pleasant, Dressing up has become a chore. You hate clothing that binds and presses on those sensitive spots from corns to collar.

Church attendance with its fellowship and inspiration may become less regular, once you discover you can listen to sermons on the air without obligation. You'd rather watch a ball game on TV than buck traffic to the stadium, gorge on peanuts and hot dogs, and yell yourself hoarse. As you watch a stage show by enthusiastic young people, your mind dwells on how much effort it must have been for them to memorize, rehearse, groom, and costume themselves, rather than on the enjoyment of the performance.

You neglect to mark your calendar and forget that you invited friends to dinner until they show up and find you gaping at TV in robe and slippers, your cupboard as bare as Old Mother Hubbard's.

Driving is no longer the pleasure it used to be. You go around blocks to avoid left turns, steer clear of freeways, give up night driving, leave keys in the ignition, and lock yourself out of the car more frequently.

You renege on a tour reservation because it's more comfortable to sleep in your own bed than to live out of a suitcase and keep pace with the crowd. The nicest part of a trip is coming home, anyway, so why not stay there?

Daily exercise demands more exertion than it used

to. Getting up out of an easy chair becomes a relativity act. You push down on the chair to rise up on your feet. You climb stairs slowly, grasping the railing firmly. Sometimes you stagger when you walk, and dizzy spells aren't unusual, making falls a risk.

The nicest thing about a stroll in the park is not the beauty of nature, the song of birds, the chatter of squirrels, the laughter of children on the playground, but the benches.

Gone is the desire to accept an office or take an active part in any organization of which you are a member.

Your lawn goes to pot, but you couldn't care less.

You still love children, but shy away from them because you can't understand their chatter.

You turn up the thermostat, the radio and the TV a few notches. Someone gives you a Bible with large print, and you grumble about the fine print they're using nowadays in magazines and newspapers.

Day by day you become more convinced that the world is going to the dogs. You know all the answers, but nobody will listen to you.

To breach the generation gap between you and your grandson, you let your hair and beard grow. But you look more like Moses than a mod guitar player, so back to the barber shop you shuffle.

You'd rather eat a donut or dry cereal and coffee for breakfast than bother to cook and to wash pots and pans. Gradually your daily diet shifts from knife-and-fork to spoon foods. Vegetables boil dry and convert to charcoal while you are talking on the phone, for your acuity is too low for you to smell them.

Insomnia has become chronic. You tend to waken around three or four in the morning to toss and turn, stretch and rub away leg cramps, traipse to the bathroom, snack on crackers and milk, recite your favorite psalm, count sheep and talk to the Shepherd, only to doze off into nonsensical dreams just before the alarm goes off.

Nothing—absolutely nothing—is as important as comfort. If you don't feel like doing something, why bother?

The Final Stage

Unless you pull up on your bootstraps or someone rescues you from apathy and lethargy, you are on your way to the third and final stage: the *my-get-up-and-go-has-gone stage*. This is the age most prominently played up by the news media. It, too, can be postponed by the precocious lovers of life.

Mildred Kinnett missed a step at a "Truth-or-Consequences" live telecast on a Jolly Sixties' outing and fractured her hipbone. Relatives, under the impression a broken hip spelled finis to active living for old folk, disconsolately disposed of her furniture and personal belongings. Mildred was eighty-six.

But after eighteen months she was released from the hospital. She rented a furnished apartment near the church. A major operation laid her low again. Then back on her feet (with a cane), she rented a single room with kitchen privileges and was soon attending church. She made eighteen aprons to send to missionaries for Christmas. Cataracts were the final millstone to shackle her. Fortunately, they are slow growing, and she has not lost her vision completely.

At ninety-four, nurses in the convalescent home where Mildred resides call her "sweety pie" and "my little white angel." They carry her from wheelchair to bed in their arms like a baby. When I told her about an expansion in the church program, her characteristic reaction was, "I'm sorry I don't have much to give anymore. But I always pray for the church."

Physically, Mildred has stepped down to the final stage. But her sweet spirit is unbent.

Adapting to the third stage of aging is effortless. By now you have learned the restful peace of silence, the euphoria of tranquillity and meditation. Albert Einstein once said, "I have never lost a need for solitude, a feeling which increases with years." As a spectator you watch the parade pass you by. You are sufficiently mature to accept it without bitterness. "To every thing there is a season," said King Solomon (Eccles. 3:1).

This is the season when Simeon and the prophetess Anna experienced the joy of seeing and identifying the Christ child in the Temple. Simeon then asked the Lord to let him depart in peace for he had seen his salvation. (See Luke 2:25-38.)

Those who have seen their salvation are ready to depart in peace when the Lord calls them home. Perhaps those who do not know our Lord are being mercifully detained a little longer to give Christians more opportunity to show them the way. The harvest is past, the summer is ended, and [they] are not saved. (See Jer. 8:20.)

Physical Caution

Chronological age does not topple us into the third stage. The criterion is whether we are able to take care of our needs unaided. Pronounced absentmindedness, chronic feelings of dejection and loneliness, dizzy spells, slight strokes, heart conditions, marked obesity, an unsteady gait, decrease in eyesight and hearing, shaky hands which drop things, arthritis which hampers essential movement are warnings that living alone is hazardous. If we fall asleep in the bathtub or when smoking, take unprescribed medicines, or if our mental alertness undulates in crests and waves, and we show a marked slowing down of reflexes we are receiving warning signals.

Accidents are the third leading cause of death among elderly people. The most frequent in the home are caused by falls, choking, poison, fires, cuts, bruises, electrocution, and running into doors left ajar.

More sinister than these health and household hazards—especially for women who live alone—are thugs, purse snatchers, extortioners, swindlers, medical quacks, and phony mail-order deals, or criminals posing as door-to-door salesmen, repairmen, and inspectors. These criminals pocket $4 billion a year through fraud, as well as endanger lives.[1]

No woman living alone should open her door to a stranger without first demanding identification. Nor should she reveal over the phone that she is alone.

A neighbor of mine was called by a stranger with a furtive, sultry voice late one night. "Are you alone?" he asked. "Oh, no! I'm not alone," she told him. "Who is with you?" he asked. "God is with me," she replied. Incredulous, he asked her to repeat what she said. "God is right here beside me," she assured him, "and He will keep you out of trouble if you ask Him to." The pest slipped noiselessly off the line and never troubled her again.

The private home among relatives may not be adequate for older members in need of physical, emotional and spiritual attention. Nursing home care or day care available in some convalescent hospitals or centers that are maintained specifically for this purpose may assist, guide and relieve a busy household in meeting these needs.

Institution Care

Being committed to an unfamiliar life-style in an institution among strangers can cause emotional shock. Some people check in elderly relatives like they would deposit a dime in a parking meter, then go their merry way. Contributing to financial support of a person in an institution does require some sacrifice, but it is no more a substitute for love and attention than child indulgence is for parental love. The gift without the giver is bare. We are by nature gregarious, and being ostracized is more painful than physical pain which can be relieved by a pill. The days are long for semi-invalids who wait for a familiar face and the touch of a hand. Unable to go where the action is, they wonder, "Where are all the people?"

How does one select a desirable convalescent or rest home—if a choice is available? First, pray that the Lord will lead you, and ask your minister for recommendations. The establishment must be licensed and accredited, fireproof, and equipped with such safety devices as handrails, grab bars, call bells or lights by beds, good lighting, and ramps for wheelchairs. Is the location convenient for frequent visits and removed from smog and noises of traffic and industries? Does the administrator have a state license? Is there a registered nurse on duty around the clock? How many patients per nurse or nurse's aid? How many patients in each room?

Ask your family physician if medical attention, physical therapy, and special diets can be relied upon; about method of purchasing medicines and about certification to participate in Medicare or Medicaid benefits.

Make an appointment to visit and check the following: How did the place smell when you entered the door? Was there a clatter of pots and pans or a noisy ventilating system throughout the building? Do employees seem cheerful and concerned about the welfare of the patients? Check the food trays, drinking water, bedding, towels, washrooms and the kitchen. Are there shampoo and barber facilities? Is there a recreation therapist with an active program scheduled? A TV in every room? An attractive dining room? Are patients content with food and service, and are they given consideration regarding compatibility of roommates? Are they permitted to enjoy their personal mementos, trinkets and wearing apparel, and do they have a place to put things? Is there a patio where they can enjoy fresh air and sunshine?[2]

Find out about visiting privileges and about extra charges not included in basic rates. And is the place under Christian management or open to churches wishing to conduct religious services?

I have visited convalescent homes with the atmosphere of a house party. Worship services, handcraft instruction, games, birthday observances, and entertainment are regularly scheduled. Visitors pass from room to room, greeting others as well as their own loved ones.

I have visited others as gloomy as a morgue; some with dusty furniture and tattletale gray linens. Once we entertained at an anniversary celebration of an institution where champagne flowed freely at a bar and was served throughout the hall and reception room. I watched a nurse pour some down the throat of a palsied patient against her pitiful attempts to remonstrate.

Visit the Sick

When you visit loved ones and other patients, identify yourself, call them by name, mention the name of the hospital and their room number, the season or date to stimulate their minds. Lead them into discussing their routine and interests. Brief them on happenings in the outside world—using good judgment, of course. To encourage communication, draw roommates into the conversation.

Take a gift—a pad and pencil, jigsaw puzzle, photos or snapshots, a flower, toilet articles, a lap cover. Take a large-print Bible and other reading matter if their vision is good, a radio with earplugs, a cassette and tapes, or just a church bulletin or pretty card. And take the children with you. (Never when they have colds.) Teach them compassion and thoughtfulness. Their presence is refreshing to old people.

Junior highs at our church accompany their Sunday School superintendents to four convalescent hospitals each month to conduct Sunday afternoon services. One girl visited an unsaved patient on weekdays also, until she led her to a personal relationship with Christ. Here is a worthy channel wherein young people can be directed to give of themselves. The slogan "Each one adopt one" is applicable with teen-agers visiting their adopted "grandparents" at regular intervals and reading to them, writing letters for them, grooming them, chatting, and encouraging them to talk. Some patients never have a visitor, nor get a letter or a gift the year round.

One Easter Sunday when the harmonica choir held services in two convalescent hospitals, a Jolly Sixties couple potted individual viola plants for everyone of the patients. How surprised and pleased they were! "Is this really for me?" some of them asked.

One church member, who doesn't sing or play an instrument, accompanies the group to visit bedfast patients and tell them about Jesus. Minnie is older than many of the patients she visits. Her knees are crippled with arthritis and cataracts cloud both eyes. Among those she has led to Christ is an eighty-two-year-old woman who had lived her entire life without Christian influence.

Though singing days may be past, music remains in the heart. One day a member of our Extension Department found a patient with an open Bible on her lap. She was humming. Bertha waited quietly for a while, then introduced herself. The patient ignored her until her soliloquy was concluded, then asked, "Couldn't you see that I was humming? Couldn't you wait?"

Bertha apologized and asked her to hum the tune

again so she could sing with her. They shared "The Old Rugged Cross."

A favorite Scripture came to Bertha's mind and she opened her Bible to Psalm 104:33,34 and read, "I will sing unto the Lord as long as I live: I will sing praise to my God while I have my being. My meditation of him shall be sweet; I will be glad in the Lord."

The patient was pleased, and they had prayer together. A nurse passing through the hall was pleased, too. "Mrs. Wood often hums, but no one has ever thought to sing with her before," she told Bertha. "Do come back again."

A patient with sparkling brown eyes always goes through the motion of directing our harmonica players at Sunday afternoon services. Delighted that our music seems to stimulate her overt response, I asked her one day if she used to direct choirs. "Yes, but not this one," she replied disdainfully. "My choirs were the finest in the country."

Footnotes

1. *Your Retirement Safety Guide,* AARP-NRTA Booklet (Long Beach, Calif.).
2. *Thinking About a Nursing Home?* American Nursing Home Associates pamphlet (Washington, D.C.)

PHYSICAL FITNESS

When we consider the three stages of our latter years it seems obvious that the get-up-and-go stage is the most enjoyable and rewarding. What can we do to keep the old Model T cruising along the highway with the motor purring? Our wheels shimmy, the fuel pump leaks, brake linings are worn thin, the headlights are dim, the air filter is clogged, and our uphostery is stained and sagged. Where do we begin?

First, have a checkup by a reliable dealer or specialist who can diagnose all operational problems. If necessary, have a complete overhaul. Then return for periodic checkups as often as indicated. Medical books on how to grow old with flash and flair read like a hi-fi needle stuck in a groove: "Start with a complete checkup—

checkup—checkup. Prevention is—vention is better—is better than no cure—no-o-o- cure."

Consult the Manufacturer's Manual frequently. Keep a driver's handbook handy regarding your own particular model for tanking up, idling, and top speed specifications.

We wouldn't fill our radiators with carbonated fluids, our batteries with alcohol, or Model-T gas tanks with the richest super-premium octane and expect our motors to purr, would we? And we'd be wise to heed those charts recommending maximum pounds of inflation and weight capacity. Loading a Model-T as though it were a semi-trailer spells trouble. The fact that a third of our contemporaries overload theirs doesn't take the drag off our springs and axles.

Medical research has established a relationship of overweight to diabetes, hypoglycemia, gout, arthritis, coronary and circulatory diseases, and less resistance to various other ailments. And think of the nurses who may sometime have to turn us over and shift us from bed to chair!

So what can we do if we're overloaded? Regard those hunger pangs as the devil's time clock. They aren't really painful. Resist them and they'll go away. Does it make sense to give microscopic taste buds on the surface of our tongues priority over an incredible aggregate of glands, membranes, muscles, fibers, juices, tubes, enzymes and valves which make up our digestive system? Half of the time we don't keep nibbling because we're hungry, but to feed our emotions. We're lonely, bored, nervous, angry, idle. Or we're afraid we can't go to sleep on an empty stomach so we "fill 'er up."

Don't be enticed by food fads, crash diets, or get-thin-quick quacks brandishing speed tactics. Get a pocket-size calorie counter. Select low-calorie, high-protein and vitamin-rich foods and cut down on salt, fats, sweets and starches to the best of your braking power. Drink water, not malts, between meals and stay out of the kitchen. Adopt an exercise schedule. Weigh yourself twice a week. Set your goal and pray for willpower.

Several years ago Victor Lindlahr wrote a best seller titled *You Are What You Eat.* Maybe he had a point. If your tank's capacity is 1500 calories and you load up with 2500, the excess thousand compresses and clogs your hoses. Three hours and twenty minutes of brisk walking could work it off, or you could take smaller portions and leave a little for the garbage disposal instead of using your stomach for one.

Diet

In the books of Moses I counted 220 verses of instructions on preparation and serving of food. God stresses proper nourishment for the body. Over and over He warned against eating fats. Most commonly consumed today are not only fat meats but solid shortenings, cream, butter, fried foods, hard cheeses, chocolate, pastries and ice cream.

God created people with perfect bodies and placed them in an idyllic setting. It wasn't long before Eve set the classic example of selecting the wrong diet for her husband and herself, with dire consequences. (See Gen. 3:16-19.)

Isaac's favorite son was Esau because the boy brought him venison. The son must have had an appetite like his dad's, for he swapped his inheritance for a bowl of stew (See Gen. 25:28-34.)

Manna sufficient for the day was provided for the nomadic Israelites. In disobedience, some hoarded double portions, only to find it wormy the next morning. Contrarily, when told to gather enough for the Sabbath on Friday, Saturday found them out with their bowls and baskets. (See Exodus 16.) They staged a demonstration for meat, and God changed the wind which brought in quail by the thousands all through the camp. The fat people stuffed themselves to death. (See Ps. 78:25-31.) Gluttons gorged themselves until meat came out of their nostrils. (See Num. 11:19,20.)

When we were children we never heard of vitamins, calories, proteins, carbohydrates, or cholesterol. We grew up on fried steaks and chops, rich gravies, eggs steeped in bacon or sausage drippings, potatoes two or three times a day, suet puddings, pastries made with lard, and corn on the cob drenched with home-churned butter. We buried cereals and fruit under sugar and rich cream. Vegetables were drowned in water—which was drained down the sink along with the nutrients—and served with cream sauce.

Now we have cholesterol and carbohydrates coming out of our nostrils, our ears, and our joints. Maybe we could remedy our dilemma if we had the willpower to eat to live instead of live to eat. Wouldn't it make sense to benefit by the Old Testament examples instead of emulating them?

Exercise

"I don't want to do nothing. I did enough in my day. I just want to sit." These were the famous last words of a woman on her way to a rest home.

Certainly we need more rest than when we were young. But disuse of muscles and joints leads to atrophy, listlessness, obesity, sluggish organs, poor coordination, and dependency upon others. Exercise we must! It's better to warm up the old motor and let it idle at the start before shifting into high gear, for a sudden spurt of jogging or weight lifting could burn out the bearings. Take it easy at first.

Exhilaration for one can be anathema for another. Gardening is widely recommended. But a lame back from raking, dizzy spells while on a ladder pruning branches, arthritic knuckles throbbing from digging weeds, and skin cancers caused by exposure to the sunlight produced nothing but a "for sale" sign on my front lawn. It took me only six months in my apartment to reduce twenty pounds and five inches of girth by limiting calorie count to 1200 daily and spending ten minutes a day in simple bending, stretching and twisting exercises. You might prefer Ping-Pong, bowling, or golf. Nine million adults bought themselves bicycles last year.

Three-wheelers and bicycles built for two are common sights at retirement haunts.

Members of a baseball team in Tucson, Arizona, all sixty or over, keep young by practicing three days a week and competing with the city's Little League team.

Of the three exercises which give the entire body the best workout—bicycling, swimming and walking—walking is the most convenient. Besides being good exercise, walking transports oxygen to the brain, broadens your environment, and gets you places. Has it ever occurred to you that Jesus walked constantly? Surely if He had owned a donkey He wouldn't have borrowed one for His triumphal entry into Jerusalem. (See Luke 19:29-40.) Here's another way to follow His example.

Does the thought of footwork make you cringe? Oh, those corns, callouses, bunions, hammertoes, ingrown toenails, fallen arches, swollen ankles, cramped muscles, and runover heels! Some feet were not made to support the weight thrust upon them. Walking to the mailbox is a chore. How can you do more?

First, get podiatric care. (Foot ailments sometimes indicate serious diseases.) Rest your feet on a stool on a level with or above your chair. Avoid crossing your legs, for this impedes circulation. Walk around the house on tiptoes. Bathe, dry, massage, cream, and powder your feet daily. Wear comfortable, correctly fitted walking shoes and change them frequently. Use a cane if you need one for balance and support. (Many a cane has served as a weapon in exigencies.)

The Israelites wandered in the wilderness forty years

without a single foot swelling (Deut. 8:4). They weren't all young. God told Moses to keep them out there until the older generation died off. (See Num. 14:34.) Take heart!

Disease

Probably our most characteristic fault in posture is sticking our necks out, resulting in a "dowager's hump" and a question mark profile. We could remedy this by drawing our stomach up under our ribs and pulling in our chins, if we start early enough. (I should have started twenty years ago. Why didn't someone tell me?) That hump can't be removed once it's there, but consistent effort might prevent further disfigurement.

Accidents

Most fatal accidents to older people occur in the home. They usually happen when we are not mentally alert or feeling up to par, our attention is distracted, or we attempt the impossible. Last year home accidents claimed 30,000 lives of folks over sixty-five. Climbing on wobbly cushions of overstuffed furniture to wash windows or hang curtains causes many a back injury. Poorly arranged furniture, clutter, unmarked steps, and stairs without railings should be corrected to avoid falls. Medicine containers should be plainly labeled to avoid poisoning. Caution should be taken to avoid fires, scalds, and burns.

Do we expect our 222 bones to rise up and march, as in Ezekiel's vision, no matter how poorly we nourish, exercise, and protect them? (See Ezekiel 37.) It's true that surgeons are performing miraculous repairs and replacements, but an accident can age us, ravage our bank account, and even cripple us for life.

A neighbor of mine walked across a freeway to an emergency phone when his car broke down, instead of raising the hood and waiting for a patrol car. He didn't make it back. Another, dressed in dark clothing, tried to cross an avenue in the middle of a block. In the twinkling of an eye these two became statistics among 2400 pedestrians sixty-five or older killed in one year.[1] And just think of what happened to Lot's wife when she didn't look where she was going! (See Gen. 19:17-26.)

The fortunate who were born strong and healthy of hardy and vigorous forebears—who are active, cheerful, confident, careful and moderate—who love life and live purposefully—need only apply their philosophy to their day-by-day living pattern.

Those who are threatened or attacked by one or more chronic diseases, take heart! Oliver Wendell Holmes—doctor, author, professor and wit who lived dynamically for eighty-five years at a time when the average life span was around forty—said that a good way to live a long life is to contract a chronic disease when young and take care of it.

Taking care of a chronic disease reverts back to that jammed hi-fi needle. Some of us don't even know if we have one! A checkup will reveal the presence of hypertension which, if not discovered and controlled, often leads to strokes, embolisms, or coronary diseases. Millions of people have diabetes and don't know it until it gets a strong foothold, though urine and blood tests are all that are necessary to discover it. Blood tests reveal a multiple of conditions—leukemia, anemia, hepatitis. . . . By now everyone should know and heed the recognized seven danger signals of cancer. Breathmobiles give free tests for respiratory disorders. Eye tests for glaucoma are given by clinics, health centers and mobile units as well as by oculists. Yet 20,000 Americans sixty-five and over lose their eyesight every year, though half of all blindness could be prevented. Ear tests indicate whether hearing could be restored by surgery or what type of hearing aid is advisable.

According to a brochure of the Arthritis Foundation, many suffer and become crippled by this affliction needlessly because they don't seek and follow medical treatment.

Because we don't see our dentists twice a year, use dental floss as well as toothbrushes methodically, nor eat a balanced diet with limited sweets and ample vitamins and minerals, cavities and diseases of gums and bone cause the loss of eighty percent of teeth in persons over thirty-five. Thirty million Americans have none of their natural ivories.[2] A consumers report states that we spend $80,000,000 on denture adhesives annually. Wouldn't "an ounce of prevention" be more economical and satisfactory than installing replacements?

Those who have missed Prevention Highway are being

enabled to detour along Control Causeway by use of such additives as digitalis, dilantin, insulin, sulfonyl-ureas, biguanides, nitroglycerin, ephedrine, or diuretics, or with transplants or pacemakers. Doctors believe there must be a remedy for every malfunction, but not all have been discovered. They also say more illnesses are psychosomatic rather than physical, caused by nega-tivism, emotional stress, anger and lack of faith.

I am inclined to believe that our earthly bodies have built-in time clocks. Our Maker has graciously installed self-healing faculties such as white blood corpuscles, antibodies and circulatory systems. We must grieve Him when we shorten our days by breaking the laws of survival through ignorance, neglect, and willfulness. Jesus never desired that anyone suffer. It was Satan who caused Job's adversities. How can we truthfully ascribe our miseries to the will of God? Yes, He tests us, but not beyond our endurance. In our weakness we should rely all the more upon His strength.

Who Cares?

Billions of dollars are being spent and hundreds of doctors and scientists are dedicating their lives to re-search in order to enable us to live long and abundant lives. What are we doing to help ourselves?

Poor old Harry, crippled with arthritis and wheezing with emphysema, sticks to his pack a day, easy chair, double helpings of pork chops, potatoes, gravy and pie. "I've never eaten a green vegetable in my life, and I don't intend to start now. Nobody is going to tell me what to do," he storms at his distraught wife.

Five-by-five Wilbert, with high-blood pressure and diabetes, has taken to alcohol.

Two women with glaucoma were warned to avoid stimulants. One said, "People with glaucoma should not drink coffee," and she doesn't. She is president of her book club. The other said, "My doctor told me not to drink coffee, but I'm not going to give it up." She is learning to read Braille. Whether drinking coffee is a deciding factor, I can't say. The point is attitude and the willpower to relinquish life patterns and habits suspected of being detrimental to our well-being.

Grandpa Bates was steeped in distress after having the last of his teeth extracted. "How many quarters did the fairies bring you, Grandpa?" little Jimmy asked. "Not one cent from the fairies, Medicare, or Blue Cross," the old man grumbled. A vision of Jimmy at his age flashed across his mind. Jimmy's generation faces a potential life expectancy of perhaps a century. Are we adults helping him build a body which will withstand stress and lead him triumphantly into the promised land? Or will our handwriting on the wall draw him into the wilderness of senility?

Some time ago I visited the Capital City Baptist Church in Mexico City where I heard a sermon on 1 Corinthians 6. Pastor Dick Shurtz brought out five points about the physical body which bear remembering: Our body is God's property (v. 13), a member of Christ (v. 15), temple of the Holy Spirit (v. 19), is designed to

114

glorify God (v. 20) and has a future through resurrection (v. 14).

Yes, the value of these old Model Ts designed by the Master Mechanic increases in direct proportion to their upkeep, like that of their counterpart. Will we allow them to depreciate by neglect? Or will we sanctify them and dedicate them to the glory of their rightful Owner?

Footnotes

1. *Your Retirement Safety Guide*, AARP-NRTA Booklet (Long Beach, Calif.).
2. Dr. John Oppie McCall, *Principles of Periodontics*, Lippincott Co. (Philadelphia, Pa. 1964).

AS A MAN THINKETH IN HIS HEART, SO IS HE

Has physical fitness any correlation with our mental processes? Daniel demonstrated the effect of body over mind by scoring topmost on a highly competitive achievement test after subsisting experimentally on a low-calorie diet. He further substantiated his premise in his account of a schizophrenic king whose sanity was restored after living seven years attuned to nature. (See Daniel 1 and 4.)

On the other hand, the mind exerts control over the body by sending messages to glands, muscles, organs and blood in strategic parts of the body. Thus doctors believe that such undesirable emotions as hatred, fear, revenge, envy, bitterness and worry cause physical illnesses. A fit of temper can trigger a heart attack as readily as pushing a hand-powered lawn mower on a hot day. But "Joy and temperance and repose slam the door on the doctor's nose."[1]

Solomon knew about the effects of thoughts and emotions on the physical body 3000 years ago, though he referred to the heart as the center of the emotions. Now that the heart as an organ has been probed, dissected, removed and transplanted, emotions as well as thinking processes are credited to the mind inside that computer at the crest of our spinal column. To take the wise king at his word: "He that is slow to wrath is of great understanding. . . . Envy is the rottenness of the bones. . . . A merry heart doeth good like a medicine, but a broken spirit drieth the bones." (See Proverbs 14 and 17.)

Mental Roadblocks

Worry negates the faith and trust of a Christian and is poison to the system. Generally it isn't the happening that breaks us; it's the way we react. If we do all we can to solve our problems, we should leave the impossible to God. With Him, nothing is impossible.

Worry is the fear of things which may never happen. A passenger on a plane which developed engine trouble mid-air kept his cool while others were biting their fingernails.

"Aren't you worried?" his young seatmate asked.

"Not really," the elderly man replied calmly. "I'm on my way to visit my son in Dallas. I have another son in heaven, and it doesn't particularly matter which one I see first."

"I wish I had your assurance," his young companion sighed.

"You can have if you put your faith and trust in God. He will take care of you."

"Then pray for me!" the girl beseeched.

"I will pray for you, but only you can invite the Saviour into your heart," the confident Christian told her.

After they both prayed, a smile lit up the young woman's face. "I'll never be afraid to fly again," she vowed.

Are we forgetful? Maybe it is fortunate that our minds are not cluttered with all that has transpired throughout a lifetime, especially incidents we regret. An eighty-year-old hospital patient confided to her pastor that she had killed a child. He drew from the depth of her soul a confession that she had induced a miscarriage by jumping up and down during an early pregnancy.

The minister's first thought was that there would be no flurry over pills, condoms, and abortions if jumping up and down would induce a miscarriage. But Sarah was in no mood for a glib retort. The feeling of guilt which she had harbored a lifetime had made her an invalid. Her memory needed healing. As he prayed for her, the minister recalled David's prayer: "Remember not the sins of my youth, nor my transgressions" (Ps. 25:7).

Then he reminded her of Saul of Tarsus who had condoned the stoning of Stephen and had persecuted Christians before his conversion, yet was able to tell the Ephesians in Acts 20:26, "Wherefore I take you to record this day, that I am pure from the blood of all men."

"You must forgive yourself, Sarah; for the Psalmist says 'Blessed is he whose transgression is forgiven, whose sin is covered.' Your sin has been covered by the blood of Jesus Christ ever since you became a Christian. You should have taken it to the Lord and left it there."

Cecil Carle, president of the board of the Alcoholism Council of the San Fernando Valley, tells of a seventy-year-old alcoholic who, in facing the question, "Is there life after death?" also asked himself, "Is there life before death?" If there was such a thing as joyous living, he wasn't getting his share. After five years of sobriety, he states his reformed philosophy thus: "Each person at any moment of his life is the result of all of the choices he has made. When one becomes dependent on alcohol, he gives up all choice every time he takes a drink. I wanted out. I had a sudden desire to live fully."[2]

Disappointments, when allowed to upset us emotionally, can cause a number of ailments, though they often turn out for our own good. Limited by our carnal nature, we cannot always comprehend what is best for us. When we neglect to ask about God's plans and purposes, we step out of His will. Like Solomon says, the ways of a man are clean in his own eyes (Prov. 16:2), and a fool's delight is in discovering himself (Prov. 18:2). We tend to become obsessed by one idea, purpose, person or object, as though life depended upon it. But God doesn't measure out just one single blessing for us. We must reach out in faith for alternatives which He holds in His hand ready for us to receive.

Reinhold Niebuhr vented a good motto in his prayer: "God grant me the serenity to accept the things I cannot change, the courage to change the things I can, and wisdom to know the difference."

Doctors say that pain can become habitual because we crave sympathy and attention rather than responsibility—like a child who develops a stomachache when he doesn't want to go to school.

We take sleeping pills because we are afraid we won't go to sleep, though it may be the very fear of wakefulness which keeps us tossing and turning. Three million people develop peptic ulcers annually which cause 12,000 deaths, and Alka-Seltzer has become a $117 million-a-year industry.

Instead of pill guzzling, maybe we'd be healthier if we'd replace negative and harmful thoughts, feelings, and actions by positive and beneficial ones before they pollute our organs. "The merciful man doeth good to *his own* soul: but he that is cruel troubleth *his own* flesh" (Prov. 11:17).

Mental Exercise

Since the mind has so much control over the body, we must keep it healthy. How? Not only with proper nutrition but by exercising it! Brain cells, like muscle tissues, atrophy with disuse. People used to think that old folk couldn't learn because the brain starts to shrink soon after we stop growing in stature. Geniuses and famous persons were exceptions. Now gerontologists tell us that few people use their full brain power anyhow, and there is plenty of reserve from which to draw.

Dr. James E. Birren, executive director of the Andrus Gerontology Center on the University of Southern California campus, says there appears to be no mental decline with age, according to new findings; that mental competence can remain high beyond the age of eighty. Whether we have limited schooling or a Ph.D., we all need to toss up new learning to sweep out the cobwebs; for human knowledge is doubling every ten years. Dr. James A. Peterson, director of liaison between the Andrus Center and AARP, says, "Older people grow in vocabulary and wisdom, but if they are not current in their thinking, their mental ability is wasted because what they think is not relevant."[3]

Seekers of mental stimulation can find a plethora of opportunities in adult schools, churches, museums, craft shops, libraries, Y.M.C.A.s and Y.W.C.A.s, art and senior citizens centers, many of which are free. Correspondence courses, documentary telecasts, and book clubs are challenging. Elizabeth Barrett Browning once said, "No man can be friendless who has God and the companionship of books."

Whether we study for a diploma, to learn a skill, or to expand our interests and knowledge, we can escape boredom for ourselves—and for those with whom we associate—by keeping mentally alert. Opportunities for study are abundant almost everywhere.

One high school, within a mile of our church, has an enrollment of 5000 in adult classes. I have taken such diverse courses as photography, Spanish, lip-reading, typing, wills and estates, creative writing, oil painting and sketching and found them all interesting and useful. Valley College issues Lifetime Gold Cards which entitle us to attend free of charge regular classes, lectures, concerts, field trips, films, plays, athletic events, festivals, and recreational activities. Local Senior Citizens Clubs have over 20,000 members. Community symphony orchestras give free concerts. One orchestra in Los Angeles is made up entirely of senior musicians.

Bible study classes are scheduled at our church several days a week. Elective courses are offered at 6:00 P.M. Sundays on varied subjects: biblical archaeology, government, hospital visitation, the Holy Spirit, bumper-sticker theology, book reviews, documentary films, and in-depth studies of books of the Bible. Our minister of bus transportation has given courses on auto mechanics for women drivers. Hobby classes are taught on week-nights. The Christian college on the church campus is now scheduling classes especially for "mature students" taught by a retired army chaplain.

Investigation may reveal equal advantages in your community. If not, demand for them should bring results. Jamestown College in North Dakota started a pioneer venture they called "Educational Vacations" three years ago. Now summer courses are being attended by retirees up to eighty-four years of age from eleven states and Canada. If you have "gone to seed" and lack self-confidence, start by auditing a class. But do the assignments secretly to get back into the groove. The struggle is worthwhile.

Bible correspondence courses are available at low cost or free through Moody Bible Institute in Chicago, the Billy Graham Association in Minneapolis, Scripture Union in Philadelphia, and Bible Fellowship in Los Angeles.

Current Needs

In three fields there is a dearth of service to older people. One is consumer education. The elderly are vulnerable to overcharging, unethical advertising, fraud, quacks, and racketeers. Consumer courses should include terminology—generic medical terms, food package labeling, and up-to-the-minute scientific vocabulary. Such jargon as virology, chemotherapy and enzymology need some groundwork for interpretation.

The second need is for an attractive and esoteric Christian magazine for seniors containing devotionals, biographies, fiction, poetry, jokes, instructive and entertaining articles, and relevant news of missions and world affairs. The magazine should be printed in large type.

The third need is for a survey and follow-up of opinions, needs, and preferences of TV programs. The television screen serves as a mirror of the outside world for many shut-ins. Next to children, retirees probably comprise the largest TV audience. More often than not, the few oldsters who are shown on the screen are emaciated sufferers of arthritis, bad breath, or "irregularity," dupes of crime, or last-stage residents of run-down rest homes.

In the meantime, let us maintain good mental health by transforming apathy, boredom, withdrawal, self-pity, worry, fear, and a poor self-image into compassion, insight, self-improvement, confidence, a sense of humor, love for others, laughter, and trust in God. "Say not thou, What is the cause that the former days were better than these? for thou dost not enquire wisely concerning this" (Eccles. 7:10).

Footnotes

1. Henry W. Longfellow, "The Rainy Day."
2. Cecil Carle, "The Progression of Alcoholism," *Van Nuys News* (Van Nuys, California, May 1974).
3. Dr. James A. Peterson, "Does Your Mind Age?" *NRTA Journal* (November-December 1971), p. 57.

Our mortal life is a one-way street from the cradle to the grave. Here we are restricted by limitations of time, space, and gravity, and enclosed within earth bodies in conformity with our environment. We are scrambled over the globe and given opportunities to manipulate and solve situations and challenges we encounter, according to our abilities and choosing.

The spiritual life is a one-way street to eternity. Eternal life is a gift of God through Jesus Christ who has gone to prepare a place for us where we shall no longer be restricted and encumbered by earthly laws and decay. When we repent and embrace Christ as our personal Saviour, He sends the Holy Spirit to be our guide. We must give Him the key to each compartment of our lives—our time, talents, and treasures—in order to attain God's peace which is beyond human understanding. We must relinquish to Him the control of our emotions, thoughts, and actions. Neglecting to turn everything over to Him is like going to a banquet to drink a glass of water, or having the talent of a great artist and spending our lives painting barns.

Are we walking in His steps? Checkups are essential to determine how we stand in our relationship with God. So, we are tested from time to time. "A living sacrifice as spoken of in Romans 12:1 has a tendency to crawl off the altar when the fire gets hot," says Pastor Dick Shurtz of Capital City Baptist Church in Mexico City.

We who have been too busy through life to grow spiritually will find our counterparts among the Hebrews in the first century A.D., "For though by this time you ought to be teachers, you need someone to teach you again the first principles of God's word" (Heb. 5:12, *RSV*). I wonder if we remind God of rats in a maze, bumping into dead ends, stumbling against obstacles, losing our sense of direction, scurrying nowhere, when all the time He is waiting for us to look up for Him to direct us.

Can we blame Him for our bungling and the bungling of our ancestors for centuries past? Man has scarred and maimed himself as well as his environment by tangling with the serpent. It must grieve God to see people suffer or He wouldn't have assured us so many times that there will be no pain or suffering in heaven.

Bible Study

We can't be wholly obedient to God without studying His Manual of Instructions. Reading the Bible is exciting, but we should always read it prayerfully to get spiritual messages back of the narratives. Read it systematically every day. Look up cross-references. Compare different versions. Be sure you have a good concordance. Read sometimes with a specific topic in mind such as prophesies, miracles, promises, salvations, biographies, moral teachings, social customs, musical instruments, birds, animals and plant life. For women's lib, bone up on queens Jezebel, Vashti and Esther. Delve more deeply into your Sunday School curriculum. Apply what you read to today's situations. If you have never read the Bible all the way through, start today.

Prayer

When you pray, you become a partner with God. Set aside a daily devotional period, preferably the first thing in the morning or right after breakfast. Be comfortable, so you can dismiss material things from your mind. Relax and meditate, to center your thoughts on the presence of the Lord waiting to communicate with you. Begin with praise and gratitude, then intercede for others: ill, needy or unsaved friends and relatives, your church, missionaries, ministers, those governing us. Make a prayer list and refer to it. Check off names as prayers are answered and add new ones as needs arise. Then pour out your own heart for guidance, forgiveness, personal needs, channels for service, an increase in grace and faith.

Prayer becomes a two-way conversation when you wait quietly for an answer. I keep a notebook beside my breakfast plate and jot down promptings I receive. Often I don't have to wait. I am interrupted! "Father, Ada has had a serious operation and. . . ." "Why don't you send her a card?" "Lord, my granddaughter is going back to college and is working to pay her expenses. She has been out of school several years and. . . ." "She has to buy textbooks. Why don't you send her a check with a note of encouragement?" "I've searched the house for music I need for a program tomorrow. Lord you know where. . . ." "You left it in your car trunk." And so it goes, day after day. It's like God told Isaiah (65:24), "Before they call, I will answer; and while they are yet speaking, I will hear."

Is returning thanks in restaurants taboo with you? It's a chance to show whose side you're on and to eat with the Lord's blessing. The other evening we noticed a black family across the dining room from us with their heads bowed. When we caught their eyes, we made the one-way sign with our fingers. After the meal we had a friendly chat and parted with a one-in-the-Spirit glow.

"I can't do anything but pray," some too weak for action bemoan. God didn't say we can move mountains if we know how to operate skiploaders and dump trucks. "Not by might, nor by power, but by my spirit, saith the Lord of hosts" (Zech. 4:6).

SECRET SERVICE

"If the shut-ins all united
In one voice of common prayer,

What a ceaseless shower of blessing
        Would be falling everywhere!

"Tho' so weak, and ofttimes helpless,
        They can wield a mighty power,
Lifting up their soul's petition
        To the Saviour, hour by hour.

"They can importune the Father,
        From the secret place and then—
In the quiet and the stillness,
        They can hear Him speak to them.

"Never soldier in fierce conflict
        Could a higher honor bring
Than the shut-in, who's performing
        Secret service for the King."[1]
                    —Gertrude R. Dugan

Church Attendance

Attending church where the gospel is preached and the Bible expounded enriches us spiritually through worship, fellowship, stewardship, music, and sermons and there is opportunity to participate in the singing. There is a personal touch; a sense of belonging.

If we live and walk in the Spirit day by day we shall reap the fruits of the Spirit which is love, joy, peace, longsuffering, gentleness, goodness, faith, meekness, and temperance (Gal. 5:22,23).

I feel fortunate for having grown up in a home where these fruits of the Spirit were exemplified. My father fit Solomon's example in Proverbs 20:7: "The just man walketh in his integrity: his children are blessed after him"; and my mother chapter 31, verse 28: "Her children rise up, and call her blessed; her husband also, and he praiseth her." Sometimes when I feel discouraged or impatient, I can still hear my mother singing her favorite song as she worked in the kitchen:

"What a treasure I have in this wonderful peace,
  Buried deep in the heart of my soul;
  So secure that no power can mine it away,
  While the years of eternity roll.

"I am resting today in this wonderful peace,
  Resting sweetly in Jesus' control;
  For I'm kept from all danger by night and by day,
  And His glory is flooding my soul.

"Peace! Peace! Wonderful peace,
  Coming down from the Father above;
  Sweep over my spirit forever, I pray,
  In fathomless billows of love."[2]

Footnotes

1. Gertrude R. Dugan, "Secret Service," from *Poems and Gospel Songs* (North Caldwell, New Jersey), p. 31.
2. W. D. Cornell, "Wonderful Peace," from *Devotional Hymns* (Chicago: Hope Publishing Company).

OUR CHILDREN'S CHILDREN

14

Our attitudes and relationships to our grandchildren range from I-raised-my-kids-and-you-can-raise-yours to parent substitution. How can we establish and maintain a healthy, happy, balanced status to squelch that overly-trumped-up generation gap? Much depends upon how dependent we are upon one another whether we live with the family or are enjoying an independent way of life far removed, whether there is only one grandchild or many, and how involved we all are with outside interests and activities. In any case, our heartstrings should be kept in tune with our children and their children. If we are separated, keep in touch by communication—correspondence, telephone, tape recordings, snapshots, gifts, visits—and through prayer for one another. If we make our home with the family, keep in tune by being tolerant without sacrificing principles, uplifting without being critical, sympathetic and kind without spoiling, able to discuss without arguing, and to merit prestige without ruling the roost. And we can do much to strengthen morale by building up single parents in the eyes of their children.

Do you tend to smother the second generation with solicitude or with austerity to compensate for your shortcomings as a parent? Think of King David, the beloved Psalmist. He let Adonijah grow up without discipline and lived to regret it, yet he has been praised three thousand years for his fine qualities. We quote King Solomon's wise sayings and tend to overlook his shortcomings as a parent. God forgives us, so we must forgive ourselves. I once expressed regret over negligence to my children and a daughter rebuked me with, "What's the matter with us? Are you ashamed of the way we turned out?" That taught me to forgive myself; to let the past be the past.

We must also be ready to forgive children seventy times seven and to compliment them for their good qualities. We must be as wise as serpents and as harmless as doves, and keep our sense of humor. For a happy, outgoing Christian has more influence on youngsters than a weeping prophet. If we show them by example that a long, useful, and rewarding life is desirable, they will see the wisdom in preparing for it physically, mentally, and spiritually. Children deprived of companionship of older persons with whom they can empathize can't be expected to project themselves into the "golden years."

My grandmother had a strong influence on me. I knew she loved me because she listened to me and showed concern for my interests and my problems. She trusted me and encouraged me to do my best. And she influenced me to accept Christ as my personal Saviour and to seek a purpose for my life.

This is a difficult age for parents to rear children, and a difficult time for children to grow up. Have we as grandparents any responsibilities? Indeed we have!

Paul told Titus that the aged women should exemplify and teach the young women in sound doctrine (Titus 2:3-5). The prophet Joel gave the old men a special message from God to extend their admonitions down to their great grandchildren (Joel 1:1-3). And the Old Testament closes with a warning about the hearts of fathers turning to the children and the hearts of children to their fathers lest God come and smite the earth with a curse (See Mal. 4:6).

Unless our Lord returns before today's children reach maturity, their mission field will present a tremendous worldwide challenge. Rapid transportation will be available from Greenland's icy mountains to India's coral strand. What can we do to help prepare their hearts for the encounter?

First of all, we can get down on our decrepit old knees and pray for them, and ask the Lord's bidding. Then put on our thinking caps. Do the toddlers have Bible story books and someone to read to them? Can the juniors name the books of the Bible in sequence and is someone helping them memorize Scripture passages?

133

Do the young people belong to study groups and do they own Bibles with a good concordance? Do they all attend Sunday School and church services? Have they set their feet on God's road?

When sophisticated young people of today find Christ, they are really turned on. They have been taught to express themselves, while in our day children were expected to be seen and not heard. Consequently, these kids can put us to shame when it comes to testifying to their peers, provided they know what and why they believe well enough to put it into words.

If all we hear in their mod music is brass and percussion, perhaps it's because we're afflicted with word deafness. Let's investigate the message and praise the Lord when unsaved youngsters respond to it.

We need to make sure that our church is firmly established upon the one Foundation or transfer to one that is, if we expect our young people to get involved. When the church comes alive for young and old, a revival should sweep the nation.

Let's take the initiative and change that noxious cliché, generation gap, to generation *grip;* and with lowliness and meekness, longsuffering, forbearing one another in love, endeavor to keep the unity of the Spirit in the bond of peace, as Paul admonished the Ephesians (4:2,3) in his epistle to them.

Explo '72 at Dallas caused me to wonder what mighty works might be wrought if a dynamic organization like Campus Crusade, which sponsored the event, were formed for retirees. Why should the old men be dreaming while the young men are seeing visions? According to a survey taken during the 1971 White House Conference on Aging, most people sixty-five and over are certain there is a God and believe in immortality. But are we too individually oriented to function as a homogeneous power if we had the leadership?

What a potential Christian army could be mustered if churches were stirred to reach and win seniors with love, conviction, and commitment! If they used their buses to bring non-drivers to church services! If they installed amplifiers for the hard-of-hearing! If they called upon the unsaved and told them the old, old story as to a little child! Nominal pew-warmers and new converts could, like the end-of-day laborers in Jesus' parable, labor on equal terms with lifetime workers.

Furthermore, what a force if effort were made to orient the 20,000,000 or so, between fifty-five and sixty-four who are retiring at the rate of 1,460,000 a year, to travel the One Way: not to toboggan downgrade, but move like a mighty army. Shouldn't we as Christians be concerned about our contemporaries who have seen but not perceived, who have heard but not understood? Maybe we are like the Laodiceans described in Revelation 3, neither cold nor hot.

Close yourself alone in a darkened room and try to imagine no Creator reflected in the beauties of nature, no heavenly Father to watch over you, no Christ who so loved the world, no Bible, no church, no divine Spirit to guide and comfort you, no one to pray to, no hope beyond the grave. On your knees, claim the promise in Galatians 3:26 that you are a child of God by faith in Jesus Christ.

Make a prayer list of your close associates who live in that darkness perpetually. Then meditate on how much you *are* doing to reach the two billion people in the world who do not yet have the gospel and how much you *could* do.

The Greek mathematician and inventor, Archimedes, said he could move the world if he had the proper tool and a place to stand. Our tool is the Word. We stand on the solid Rock. What's stopping us?

Thousands of those teen-agers who stormed the Dallas Cotton Bowl for Christ in '72 went there on a shoestring, while 90 percent of *us* have a dependable "cruse of oil that never runs dry"—from a drip to overflowing proportions. True, 30 percent of our nation's poor are in our age bracket, but many are the ways that the Lord can be served without a fat purse.

On the other side of the coin, 30 percent of the most affluent Americans are in the upper age bracket. Oldsters contribute a hefty figure to the $43 billion Americans spend annually on recreation, alcohol, and tobacco. Look in on Las Vegas and you'll note our vintage at bars and game tables. Our yen for outboards figured substantially in the $3.9 billions spent by recreational boaters last year. One and six-tenths billion dollars were spent on pet foods in 1973 compared to $192 million for foreign missions.[1]

Don't get me wrong. Retirees have a right to live life to the hilt. Like POWs returning home, our first thought is, "At last, I am free!" Once accustomed to being free, our next thought is, "Free for what?" Only egoists can remain insensitive to responsibilities, brotherhood and altruism indefinitely. To a person with an active mind, a perpetual vacation lapses into fiddling while Rome burns rather than living abundantly. A worker from the labor force declines rapidly if he allows his muscles to get flabby and his regular habits to degenerate into thumb twiddling. Retirement for an executive or professional person can be traumatic. Loss of identity and purpose is a morale killer. Achievement and purpose

are psychological needs with therapeutic value to the server.

Retirement can be a psychological time for spiritual regeneration; a time for rebirth; a time to forget those things which are behind and press toward the mark of high calling of God in Jesus Christ, like the apostle Paul resolved to do (Phil. 3:13,14). Persons with talents and skills, such as artists, writers, inventors, construction workers, teachers, scientists, engineers, doctors and nurses are especially needed in fields of service all over the world. (See Appendix.)

Pray

If you have not committed yourself to some specific field of service, you can start a spiritual awakening within your own four walls by exercising your potential prayer power. Pray for the Holy Spirit to direct your life. Pray for the church. Pray for the leaders of our country. Pray for a moral and spiritual awakening in America and beyond our borders. You don't have to be rich, healthy or handsome to become a partner with God through intercessory prayer.

Faith Chao, co-organizer and administrator of Chinese for Christ, with her missionary husband Calvin, whose chief ministry is to Chinese students in the United States, started a prayer league now numbering 20,000 prayer warriors scattered over the globe. Says Faith: "China was lost to Communism because Christians, as a whole, failed to pray. I am a Chinese burdened to pray for America because I see things happening in America today just as they happened in China. My heart laments to see the United States going spiritually downhill. Only God can deliver this country from destruction. Won't you pray with me?" (Chinese for Christ, Box 29126, Los Angeles, Calif. 90029.)

Will we? Do we? And why not reciprocate by praying for Faith's homeland? Did you know that the Far East Broadcasting Company (Box 1, Whittier, Calif. 90608) is beaming the gospel into mainland China by radio—the only open door since 1949—and that you can sponsor a weekly or monthly 15-minute program for $5.00? Not only to China, but over any of twenty-three stations in forty languages and dialects.

Jeremiah Calvin Lanphier, a layman in a church about to close its doors in 1857, started a prayer movement with only six men which lasted twenty years and won a million converts.[2] The Holy Spirit is as powerful today as He was then, if we yield to His control.

Study Scriptures

The nationwide movement of cottage Bible study groups is an informal means to expand Bible literacy and show your neighbors the way of salvation. Meetings can be discussion sessions or teaching situations. Open with a short prayer and a Psalm, then concentrate on one of the Gospels. Should denominational or sect controversies arise, solve them with Dr. John Haggai's axiom: "No man is entitled to any opinion on any moral or spiritual question where God has spoken."[3]

Most Christian magazines contain Bible study lessons. Correspondence courses for home-study groups and also films and filmstrips are available from the Moody Bible Institute (820 North LaSalle Street, Chicago, Illinois 60610). The Navigators (Colorado Springs, Colorado 80901), publish helpful material including a ten-unit series called "Studies in Christian Living," and also have a catalogue of reel and cassette tapes. Correspondence courses for individuals may be adapted to group study, available from Moody, Navigators, The Bible Fellowship in Los Angeles at 10801 Wilshire Boulevard (90024) and Scripture Union, 1716 Spruce Street, Philadelphia, Pennsylvania 19103.

Distribute Tracts

Distributing tracts, carefully selected as to subject and content, is an effective ministry. Leave one with a tip for the waitress when you eat out. Hand one with payments to salespersons and service station attendants. Share them with seatmates on buses, discussing them when circumstances permit.

To old-timers like me, "colporteur" conjures memories of an itinerant horseback rider galloping across the plains with a saddlebag filled with Bibles. Volunteer colporteurs today are distributing Bibles and other Christian literature for the American Bible Society and the Pocket Testament League to homes, hospitals, and rest homes.

Support Causes

At last you have time to take a Christian stand against graft, crime, pornography, and subversion by writing your convictions to representatives in all branches of government and supporting qualified Christians in office.

Even those of us with physical handicaps can "go into all the world" vicariously. One evening when the Korean Children's Choir gave a concert at our church, I sat with a multiple-handicapped retired schoolteacher and WAC. I plugged her earphone into the sound system so she could hear the music. Beulah is a blind diabetic who has to inject insulin into her system daily. A few weeks after the concert this woman who had never married proudly showed me a snapshot of a Korean orphan she had pledged to support and asked me to describe to her this child she could not see.

"I never thought it could happen to me," she said with tears of joy streaming down her face. "At last I am a mother!"

Volunteer Service in the United States

Are you footloose and ready to broaden your horizon? Maybe you have sung, "I'll go where you want me to go, dear Lord," all of your life. And just maybe God is extending your life-span so that you can keep that promise. Pensions can be mailed to you wherever you hang your hat for a specified period of time. Volunteer

service doesn't always require full time. There may be opportunity for sightseeing and for making new friends.

Gospel Recordings Incorporated (122 Glendale Blvd., Los Angeles, California 90026) operates as though contemporary living were not controlled by the monetary system. Technicians, machinists, carpenters, stenographers, printers, photographers, artists, and maintenance crew serve without salaries by faith or on retirement income. Retired volunteers find living quarters near the plant and work one to five days a week. The gospel is recorded in some 3800 tongues. GRI is a worldwide missionary organization with branch offices scattered over several continents, and cooperates with all recognized evangelical denominations and societies by supplying gospel records free of charge.

Mr. and Mrs. Walter Lewis sold their farm in Ohio and moved to Los Angeles after "catching the gleam" during a vacation period spent in service. "We count it a privilege to send out the gospel to the ends of the world by means of records," says Walter, "and to work with people of like faith."

Five thousand Laubach literacy volunteers are tutoring adult illiterates in nearly every state in the Union in reading, writing, and conversing in English. To qualify you do not have to be a trained teacher. Instruction is provided by the National Affiliation of Literacy Advance in local church, civic and service buildings. Volunteer writers are also needed to prepare literature on a mid-elementary grade level.

Gene and Bettie Novinger of Newport News, Virginia retired early from rewarding positions to become literacy missionaries. They were sent to New Mexico to tutor Mexican-Americans in a Spanish-speaking Southern Baptist church. (Neither of them could speak Spanish.) Gene has established other centers in New Mexico, Texas and California. They have time for their hobbies, music and lapidary, and for volunteer service in a local hospital one day a week. They live entirely on their retirement income. "God can use our bonus years if we commit ourselves," Bettie assured me. "Our life is rewarding and fulfilling."

Campus Crusade for Christ, with headquarters at Arrowhead Springs, California is oriented to serve youth, but senior adults serve Campus Crusade in many capacities at home and abroad. John and Florence Haffner feel that serving the Lord in a Christian atmosphere and being a part of world evangelism, based upon Bill Bright's widely circulated, "Four Spiritual Laws," are ample rewards. John is a film technician. Florence is a retired teacher serving in the audio-visual department.

Numerous and diverse are the fields for Christian volunteers who make themselves available, in addition to opportunities within home churches. Some require special talent and training. All require dedication to the Lord and a desire to serve and uplift humanity. (See Appendix for a broader list of opportunities, and contact your denominational home mission board. I make no claim to have all of the answers.)

Be a Missionary

Volunteer service abroad is exotic and broadening. Age is venerated in most foreign countries. Retired ministers, denominational workers, and volunteers with skills mentioned previously in this chapter have the widest choice of fields. Lacking special training and qualifications, our duties may be labor and routine, such as housekeeping, child care, gardening, maintenance, sewing, "paper work," or medical assistance. Read 1 Corinthians 12 and 13 daily for a week before making a decision. And can you shake a black, brown, red or yellow hand as cordially as a white one? You will discover that ours is a minority race.

We should still be in the get-up-and-go stage, healthy enough to be an asset, capable of adjusting to a new way of life and not an easy prey to "culture shock," free of pride, prejudice, and irascibility. We must be spiritually mature, patient, adaptable, cooperative, and conscientious, anxious to free the career missionaries to concentrate on carrying out their commission.

If you have never traveled abroad, apply for a short term or take a mission tour first. Such a trip will enlarge your friendship circle, expand your horizon, and humanize your concept of missions. If you decide you are not suited for a longer assignment, your heart will prompt you to help finance needs you have seen with your own eyes. Once you witness a voodoo ceremony and the appalling sight of homeless people sleeping on sidewalks in Haiti—experience the crowded condition of Enrico Garey's tiny chapel in Campeche where he preaches and teaches descendants of the pagan Mayas—or once you meet a born-again deaf graduate student in Jamaica and hear how, as a lad, he was found by a missionary, living with a herd of goats on a hillside and had never communicated with a human being—you will gladly relegate assumed necessities to the nonessential category and contribute toward spreading the good news and meeting basic needs of these faraway people who have tugged at your heartstrings. When you enjoy the hospitality of an English-speaking church on the other side of the globe you will never again share Elijah's thought that you and your home church or denomination alone never bowed the knee to Baal.

Mission Tours Abroad

Ministers, missionaries, and seasoned lay travelers are organizing and conducting mission tours with the cooperation of local travel agents, airlines, tour wholesalers, consultants on their foreign mission boards, and missionaries on the fields to be visited.

Donald Penney, a Conservative Baptist missionary on furlough, took a group to his mission field in Africa with stopovers at points of interest. Rev. Calvin Chao of Chinese for Christ conducted a summer tour to Taiwan. The American tourists lived in Christ College dormitories, participated in a seven-day evangelical conference and visited tourist attractions. A CBFMS representative conducted a 20-day tour of mission fields in South America. Pastor Wilfred Moore of the First Baptist Church of Amarillo, Texas has led lay church members on personal evangelism crusades to Japan, Korea, Africa, Mexico, and Malaysia. Retirees have participated enthusiastically on work tours to mission fields.

Some tour agencies which set up custom-made tours to be conducted by Christian leaders are: Gotaas World

Travel, 7 West Madison Street, Chicago, Illinois 60602; Menno Travel Service, 800 Second Avenue, New York, N.Y. 10017; and Universal Travel Service, Inc., Countryside Mall, Box 874, Palatine, Illinois 60067. Compassion, Inc., Box 880, Blenheim, Ontario, Canada, conducts tours to their mission fields in the Orient. Sightseeing is included.

Rev. Herb McComas of World Missions Tours (P.O. Box 515, Miami Springs, Florida 33166) has been conducting orientation tours to India, Africa, the Holy Land and Middle East, Haiti, and Latin America ever since 1963—Christian witness crusades, gospel music caravans, and short-term work camps. Churches, schools and clinics have been built. Tons of medical supplies have been shipped and dispensed overseas. More than a hundred WMT tourists have responded to calls for full-time service.

I joined a recent tour to Guatemala and Honduras. We took in the usual tourist attractions, but slept and ate most of the time at mission headquarters. We passed out tracts in Spanish at open markets, and spent evenings and weekends singing, playing, witnessing and conducting services in churches and branch missions. Paul Enyart, administrative field secretary, was in charge to establish rapport and interpret. The group was from the Friends Church and the tour director was a Methodist minister; but this Baptist has rarely experienced the spiritual benediction we shared that last night. Crowded into a hotel room at beautiful Lake Atitlan for our final Bible study, we took hands and sang, "Blest be the tie

that binds our hearts in Christian love. The fellowship of kindred minds is like to that above."

At Wycliffe Bible Translators Center in Guatemala City, I was hosted by a retired school librarian from Kansas. This is Beth Studebaker's sixth year serving Wycliffe. In Mexico City, I met Jack Baskins serving in public relations at the Wycliffe Institute. The Baskins closed out a profitable business in Colorado in answer to God's call into volunteer service. Doris Galpine, a retired secretary from Bothell, Washington went to the

Wycliffe base in Colombia, South America to take on secretarial duties.

Being a linguist is not essential to serve Wycliffe. Piloting planes, keeping books, teaching missionaries' children, typing, doing construction and maintenance work disencumbers the translators. Wycliffe uses 6000 volunteers in twenty-two countries where dialects are recorded, an alphabet devised, Scriptures are translated, and people are taught to read the good news in their own vernacular.

When I was in Bethlehem, I was impressed by a great institution overlooking Shepherds' Field, partly because its management exemplifies "Senior Power." An American minister, the Rev. Ralph Baney, founded Holy Land Christian Mission for orphans and crippled children in 1936. Under his thirty-six years of management, eighteen buildings were constructed, including a home for 500 orphans and an orthopedic hospital accommodating 200 crippled children. Ill health ultimately forced Rev. Baney to lay his cloak upon the shoulders of a 78-year-old minister, the Rev. Lyndon Harper, who had only a few months previously superseded 85-year-old Dr. Frank Field as president of the Board of Directors. Dr. Field continues his twenty-year affiliation as president emeritus. Still another octogenarian, Albert Arnold, at eighty-seven, flew to Bethlehem from North Carolina for the dedication of a new hospital for which he donated an imposing tower. A widow of seventy-four flew over from Florida to fill the post of supervisor in the crippled children's dormitory.

The staff at the mission are also showing compassion for hundreds of widows and refugees who live in cold, dark rooms, caves, lean-to's, hovels and shacks in the area. They have no social security, no families to support them, no opportunities for employment. Since 1968, five hundred of these people have been recipients of the Holy Land Mission Widow and Refugee Aid Program, through the benevolence of Americans like you and me. In addition, baskets containing food and the Gospel of Mark are distributed to hundreds of other needy during the Christmas season. "These are some of the most destitute people on the face of the earth," Rev. Harper told me.

The world is the field in which we could enlarge the place of our tents and stretch forth the curtain of our habitation (Isaiah 54:2) while we are free, at the peak of our skills and blessed with reasonably good health.

151

Hundreds of retirees are participating enthusiastically on work tours and on longer assignments at mission fields all over the world. "It would require more than 16,000 people to fill all the job openings," says Irving Philgreen, executive director of Short Terms Abroad.

Edwin L. Frizen, Jr., executive secretary of Interdenominational Foreign Mission Association of North America, writes: "Retired persons can make valuable contributions to missionary outreach around the world. Much more so, in fact, than many of the young people who go for very short terms. Many of our current opportunities could certainly be filled by them."

Norman Cook of Overseas Crusades tells of gratifying associations with senior adults in their upper seventies and eighties.

Christian Service Corps operates on the belief that every Christian should give two full years to the Lord's work.

Life is a vapor "that appeareth for a little time, and then vanisheth away" (Jas. 4:14). The undetermined length of time before we vanish away is but a moment to lay at the Master's feet.

Footnotes

1. *Facts and Figures*, Interdenominational Foreign Mission Association, Ridgefield Park, New Jersey 07660 and *National Enquirer*, Sept. 1974, Lantana, Fla. 33460.
2. William Miedema, *The Prayer Meeting That Shook America* (El Dorado Park Community Church, Long Beach, Calif.).
3. John Haggai, *Straight from the Shoulder*, Evangelism International, Atlanta, GA.

My friend Bea, who introduced me to the Jolly Sixties, had a relinquishing attitude toward life and death. Bea was not a sentimental person and wanted no pity. I believe that only two of her best friends knew that she had undergone two operations for intestinal cancer and had been told that a recurrence would be fatal.

In the hospital she read, listened to her transistor radio, and chatted with visitors and nurses as though she were on a vacation. "This is the life!" she beamed. "I'm attached to so many cables I don't even have to eat."

She evaded serious discussions with her friends about her condition right up to the time of her death. Or was it her friends who evaded the subject? Why do Christians cringe from discussing impending death? We claim to sorrow not, even as others who have no hope (1 Thess. 4:13), and sing jubilantly, "I am bound for the promised land."

Ministers and hospital chaplains know best how to broach the subject; but we shouldn't discourage a dying friend from sharing with us how it feels to face death. He may fear isolation more than death itself, and being given the opportunity to tell about the experience may give him emotional release.

James W. Hoffman, in an article, "How to Decide What to Tell a Loved One Who Is Dying" in *Today's Health* (February, 1972), says "What people think they think about death is not how they really feel when they face it." He quotes one patient as saying, "I felt the urge to let go. It was beautiful, and there was no pain." A patient with bone cancer invited friends and relatives to a "going away party" and told them, "I have a date way up there with God. Today is my happy day." A psychiatrist at Stanford University School of Medicine has a forum for dying patients so they can discuss their thoughts, conditions, and feelings. He believes that sharing will help to counteract "the usual silent conspiracy of the outside world."

I believe that Bea wanted to die with dignity and without emotional demonstration. She was ready to meet her Lord and faced the inevitable with faith and confidence. Nevertheless, I was shocked when Dave didn't cancel a Jolly Sixties social that fell on the same day as her funeral.

"We must live for the living," Dave told me. "Life must go on, though we pass away one by one. Bea would not want the social cancelled." Of that I was certain.

Jolly Sixties accept death as the normal termination

of mortal life, and the passageway to life everlasting.
At peace with the Lord, we need not fear death. However, we sorrow over the loss of our loved ones and
express sympathy to others in their grief. Widows and
widowers need the consolation of those who understand
the shock, loneliness, and depression they suffer. Social
isolation can be more painful than death.

In 1960, the newly organized Jolly Sixties helped to
assuage this sorrow of a charter member who has served
as corresponding secretary for fourteen years. Dollie
Reed penned this poem, at the death of her husband.

VICTORY OVER DEATH

"Oh, grave, where is thy victory?
Oh, death, where is thy sting?
Since Jesus died upon the cross
No fears will dying bring.

"He bore the nail prints in His hands,
The crown upon His brow;
He paid the price that set us free.
You cannot harm us now."

When members of our group die, the Jollies travel
by church bus to the funeral. The organization presents
memorial gifts of books or filmstrips to the church library in the name of the deceased.

Sometimes our ministers conduct a memorial service
for a stranger in the community and we are asked to

attend, lest the funeral chapel be empty, to give comfort to the bereaved. Our men act as pallbearers.

One day when Dave drove a bus load to Forest Lawn in Hollywood Hills, I pointed out my lot. "Will you bring a busload of Jollies to my funeral?" I asked him.

I was taken aback by his genial reply. "I'll be delighted!"

"Have a nice day!" I quipped back. "I won't be with you."

"Righto!" he agreed.

David knows his sheep and directs his jibes at those blessed with a sense of humor.

Once I took my fifth-grade class to Forest Lawn in Hollywood Hills to see the great Venetian glass mosaic picture, "Birth of Liberty," and the replica of the Old North Church, where Paul Revere hung his lantern. I decided that this would be a pleasant place for my loved ones to meditate, so I purchased a burial space.

I was given a memorial record book in which to list vital statistics, names and addresses of those I wanted to be notified, and detailed plans for my memorial service. To spare my children the lavish expenditure for a steel or bronze casket with silver-plated handles and velvet lining to be buried in the ground, I indicated a cloth covered one in gray or pink. Yes, pink!

I resisted inducement to buy a funeral service policy. Money paid for such a policy is buried indefinitely without interest. And there is no guarantee against increase in funeral cost when the time comes. I believe that my Social Security, teachers' death benefits and maybe a little insurance money should suffice.

Plan a Funeral

Next to a home and a car, a family's largest investment can be in a funeral if no plans are made until the exigency arises. The need often follows a protracted and costly illness. If the deceased has expressed no desires regarding final procedures, a multiple of decisions including financial arrangements must be made in haste under emotional strain—a circumstance which increases the cost and the eventuality of regrets. Yet we all know that "it is appointed unto men once to die" (Heb. 9:27), and approximately 1,900,000 Americans keep this appointment every year.

Burdened with grief, the bereaved must arrange for the removal of the body from the hospital or home, a place of burial, a place for funeral or memorial service, and must set the date and time. Will it be public or private? Open or closed casket? They must notify family, friends, organizations and news media.

An obituary must be prepared, and accommodations arranged for visiting relatives. Details such as pallbearers, minister, musicians, burial clothes, viewing room, hearse and limousines, embalming and cosmetic restoration, choice of Scriptures and songs all must be settled simultaneously. To these burdens add concern about financial charges, credit, the sealing of safe deposit boxes and a court injunction tying up bank accounts.

In 1957 a group of people in Los Angeles concerned

about the exorbitant cost of funerals formed a nonprofit funeral society, whose aims are economy, simplicity and dignity in funeral arrangements. Now there are societies throughout the United States and Canada which have agreements with local funeral directors and reciprocal arrangements for transfer of membership. (For more information, write to the Continental Association of Funeral and Memorial Societies, Suite 1100, 1828 L St. N.W., Washington, D.C. 20036.)

Entombment or Cremation?

Burial has been the accepted means of placing the body at rest in most Christian nations ever since the apostolic age. "But if the Spirit of him that raised up Jesus from the dead dwell in you, he that raised up Christ from the dead shall also quicken your mortal bodies by his Spirit that dwelleth in you" (Rom. 8:11; see also 1 Cor. 15). God buried Moses in the land of Moab. Sarah and Abraham were buried in a cave. The kings Manasseh and Amon were buried in the royal garden, Samuel in his house. Joseph's body was embalmed, placed in a coffin, and his bones carried from Egypt to Canaan many years later.

Both burial and cremation seem to be as old as time. Do we associate cremation with Hinduism and Buddhism and burial with Christianity and Judaism? In ancient China, interment was symbolic of attachment of the people to mother earth. On the island of Bali, the funeral pyre is believed to release the soul. The bodies of Saul and his three sons were burned, then buried under a tree. Abraham said, "I am but dust and ashes" (Gen. 18:27). As far back as 1549, "earth to earth, ashes to ashes, dust to dust, in sure and certain hope of the resurrection" was included in the liturgy of the Anglican church.

With population density increasing, urban cemeteries filled, and more space needed for the living, the practice of cremation is gaining, notably in European cities. It is claimed that cremation is more sanitary than entombment, particularly in cases of contagious disease. The cost is about a third unless the body is first embalmed for the memorial service. Interment is impractical where water level is high, as in New Orleans, Amsterdam, and Venice, and also in the Arctic Zone where ground is permanently frozen.

Everyone should indicate his or her preference during lifetime, and not leave the decision to others.

When I scheduled my hundredth plane flight, "land-lubber" friends asked if I was ever afraid to fly. "I'd as soon meet my Lord in the air as on the freeway," I told them. In such an event my body might be cremated instead of resting in a pink casket, but I am confident that my spirit would safely soar beyond the blue.

As a choir director in my earlier days, I supplied music for funerals of church members and was frequently in contact with death. I do not agree with Solomon that the day of death is better than the day of one's birth. But I do not entertain a morbid concept of death. I may never finish my course like Paul did, and my innate curiosity about unfinished business may be suspended midair.

But I have a deeper curiosity about the hymn Jesus sang with His disciples after the Last Supper. I wonder if it was similar to the "Doxology" or "Bless Be the Tie that Binds." Was it an ancient Hebrew chant? Or one of David's psalms? Surely Jesus must have sung the lead. James and John perhaps sang tenor, while Andrew and Bartholomew carried the bass. Peter, in my imagination, was slightly off pitch without being aware of it. Was there pathos or was there triumph in our Lord's voice ere He strode the path to Gethsemane? I feel sure He will satisfy my curiosity one day by telling me all about it. Perhaps He will teach me the hymn. He restored the servant's ear after impetuous Peter severed it that night. I am sure He will restore both my voice and hearing acuity.

Prepare a Will

It is estimated that $100 million is wasted every year by Christians who die without leaving a will. A person who fails to make a will turns over his lifetime accumulated possessions to the state. In the red tape of probate courts, the residue ultimately is distributed according to state rulings after passing through state appointed administrator, lawyer, appraisers, bankers, tax assessors, and the court. Doesn't that seem as slothful as burying our possessions in the ground? Neglecting this responsibility brings further anguish to bereaved families.

Upon reading about the trials a widow of a renowned celebrity went through because her husband neglected to make a will, I resolved to save my children from undergoing her heartrending experiences. His checking account was frozen, insurance policies sealed in a safe deposit box by an Internal Revenue Service ruling. An appraisal was required of her husband's personal items, from power tools to speeches. And she had to go through costly and lengthy court action. I had an attorney prepare my first will, and every time I make a business transaction or change my mind, I rewrite it and destroy the previous one.

Unless you own only a modicum of household furnishings and personal items, it is advisable to hire an attorney to write up your will. It's his business to know how. You may not be able to prepare a will that can stand up under legal tests any more than you can repair a motor, tailor a suit of clothes, compose a song, build a house, or paint a portrait. Maybe you can, and maybe you can't.

King David was certainly a knowledgeable and literate person. Yet he bungled matters when he expressed his desire to have Solomon succeed him only by word of mouth. Or maybe he did not use legally accepted terms. Or he failed to have proper witnesses. Anyhow, after Absolom and Adonijah both attempted to usurp the throne, causing much bloodshed and David's abdication, David took Nathan's advice and made a formal decree before a priest, a prophet, and the captain of his bodyguard. (See 2 Sam. 15:1-17; 1 Kings 1:5-40.)

In Jesus' parable of the vineyard, sharecroppers plotted to kill the landowner's son and heir, mistakenly thinking they would thereby inherit his property. (See Mark 12:1-8.)

Don't rely upon your children to portion out your worldly goods. The state has preemption over anyone but yourself. Besides, many a distant relative, in-law, or self-appointed counselor has dropped a fly in the ointment. Unlike David, you won't be around to clarify ambiguities or settle disputes.

What to Include

Whether you hire a lawyer or do it yourself, you should first take an inventory and evaluate everything you own, and decide to whom you wish to devise each item. Such a list often amazes even one who considers himself poverty-stricken. Old pewterware, cut glass, needlework, a stamp or coin collection, books out of print, porcelain figurines, Colonial stoneware, Bavarian china, an old piano stool, an heirloom clock may be valuable antiques or collectors' items.

Familiarize yourself with state requirements, and if you move to another state, repeat the performance. Your will must include your name and address, the statement that you are of sound mind and memory, that you are not acting under duress or undue influence of any person, and that it is your last will and testament and it revokes all other previous wills. You order that just and legal debts be paid out of your estate. You clearly designate names and addresses (and usually relationship) of persons and organizations to whom you bequeath legacies, and exactly what you want them to have. You should provide legal descriptions of real estate property.

Nominate and appoint a competent and available executor or executrix and also a substitute, experienced in business management. If they are members of your family, close friends, or associates, you will probably request that no bond or other security be demanded of them.

Your signature with the date must be witnessed by two or three adults not named as beneficiaries. Even having the pastor of the church you espouse sign as a witness might void the document. Select witnesses with normal life expectancies beyond your own. You need not permit them to read your will.

A holographic (in longhand) document should remove doubt that you executed it, but if legibility is dubious, accompany it with an *identical* typed copy. In some states a holograph will is not legal. Any erasure or correction voids the document. Start over!

Immediate relatives not named in the will are not bound by it. Some advise that we either state that we leave them no bequest (perhaps stating why) or leave them one dollar. I included the following provision: "If any legatee objects, contests, or aids in contesting any provision in this will I annul my bequest herein made to such beneficiary, and request that his or her share be apportioned to my other children in equity."

Other Considerations

Some authors of books and articles say we should specify everything we own in a will. Others advise not to lengthen and complicate the document with such particulars as clothing, linens, books, household items, funeral arrangements, life insurance policies, and joint accounts with right of survivorship. It is better to write a letter with detailed instructions to your spouse, or other member of your family. Discuss everything in a matter-of-fact way, and inform him or her where to locate the will, insurance policies, tax records, automobile pink slip, birth and marriage certificates, and dated receipts of sizable purchases to facilitate appraisal. File these papers in a fireproof strongbox or combination safe in your home or place of business, where they won't be sealed when they are needed. You are more likely to keep documents updated if they are readily available.

What are an executor's duties? Here are a few. Notify heirs and read the will to them. Publish notices in newspapers to inform creditors. Secure certified copies of the death certificate for insurance companies and Social Security. Pay debts and get releases. Pay funeral expenses. Update deceased's income tax. Settle estate taxes, if any, after totaling assets, et cetera, et cetera.

What about probate? Probate is the official proving in court that a will is authentic and valid. Estates valued at a few thousand dollars may be handled by the County Treasurer if unchallenged. Probate may be essential when a person dies without having made a will and the court has to appoint an administrator and officiate.

164

Also, when persons move from state to state, or, when heirs live in states other than the deceased's residence, when the deceased owns property in other states, when heirs cannot be located or have died, when there is a second marriage with no prenuptial financial contract and disputes arise concerning children of former marriages, when death of testator and sole beneficiary is simultaneous and the will does not contain a simultaneous death clause, and when estates are large enough to require federal taxes. (They begin at $60,000 and soar from 3 to 77 percent.) Probate renders a legatee's title to inherited real estate unchallenged.

Probate is costly, long drawn out, and differs from state to state. One of the nation's great needs is a Uniform Probate Code. One has been defined and adopted by a few states, but only public demand is likely to bring about universal adoption.

If this all sounds complicated, it is! The above information is as much to show when there's need for professional service as to tell how to do it. You might get some guidance from your insurance agent, your minister, a trust officer in your bank, a tax accountant, or, back to the original tune, an attorney. Never from a stranger or a volunteer know-it-all.

When 75 to 80 percent of us allow the state by default to make our wills, when we leave funeral planning to be done in three grief-stricken days, is it any wonder that funeral and probate costs are excessive? Every week $86 million are buried in probate. Improperly and carelessly made wills are largely responsible for heirs never knowing about their estates. Billions of dollars are waiting to be claimed.

Bequests Other Than Worldly Goods

Oddly, the most deficient part of my anatomy will be useful after I am gone! I have willed my temporal bones to the Ear Bank of Los Angeles Foundation of Otology for research on hearing and balance disorders, to benefit future generations. Removal of the inner ear structure will not disfigure the outer ear, I am assured. There are ear banks in other parts of the country. Other organs and the entire body may benefit science after we have cast them aside. Upon acceptance, medical schools and organ banks supply identification cards and detailed instructions.

Your Stewardship a Heritage

There are means whereby we can contribute financially to the Lord's work after we have departed, too. Consider life insurance, for example. Life insurance proceeds are generally payable in cash immediately, free from taxes and probate. Have you thought about naming your church, missions, or a predilected institution as beneficiary to an existing policy? Or as secondary, remainder, residual, or co-beneficiary? Or taking out a new policy? Under certain conditions your premiums will be tax deductible. This will enable you to provide a sizable lump sum scholarship fund or a memorial gift. If you are now receiving dividends, would lowering your income bracket be beneficial? Assign them to your church!

Check your insurance policies and discuss the matter with a reliable agent. "You don't need to be rich to give substantially, because life insurance multiplies your money," says Ed Welge, administrator and director of finance at the First Baptist Church of Van Nuys. Church members should be praying about this type of stewardship, nor should we wait until we have passed our best earning years. "Blessed are the dead which die in the Lord . . . their works do follow them" (Rev. 14:13).

Perhaps you have a living trust to provide you with a lifetime income which could be converted to a ten-year certain plan and leave a residual sum for stewardship if you do not live out the ten years.

Are you a loner? And are your checking and savings accounts solely in your name? Would you rather they go to the state—or to your church—if you should suddenly be called home? By placing your accounts in trustee or joint tenancy with right of survivorship with your church finance administrator, your church would benefit, and there would be someone who could withdraw funds for you in case you become incapacitated.

Some elderly Christians with a surplus prefer to watch their money build youth centers, orphanages, hospitals, missions or schools rather than leave bequests for the veiled future. They establish memorials or adopt an *inter vivos* program of planned giving.

Rev. Dale Scott tells about an elderly convert who went down into the baptistry with his wallet clasped between his hands. Questioned about it, he explained, "I have worshiped the almighty dollar all of my life. Now I want to dedicate my money as well as myself to Christ."

Footnotes

1. "Four dying outpatients meet weekly, discuss their plight," *Grit*, Dec. 23, 1973.

THE GATE KEEPER 17

Jesus broached the subject of His death a number of times, but His disciples didn't want Him to talk about it. There are some like them in many families today. A husband or wife who has this attitude may suffer unnecessary hardship; especially a surviving wife, whose husband carried responsibilities on his shoulders and failed to prepare his wife to assume them.

When Peter presumed to hush-hush Jesus' candid efforts to prepare His disciples for His death, his Lord called him "Satan." Satan brought death into the world, and Christ was about to overpower death. Even today, we take Peter's stance. Do we think if we ignore death it will go away?

Dying is not always accompanied by pain. Paul told the Romans (8:18), "The sufferings of this present time are not worthy to be compared with the glory which

169

shall be revealed in us." Medications are available to relieve pain, today. Jesus was offered a sedative, but He refused it. Our death pangs cannot compare with His suffering for us.

Power in the Blood

What if Jesus had died without shedding His precious blood on the cross for us? What would be our condition today if He had drowned when the disciples asked if He didn't care if they perished in that storm at sea? If the threat to stone Him in the Temple or on Solomon's Porch had been enacted? If the Jews at Nazareth had succeeded in throwing Him over the cliff? If the soldier had obeyed orders to break His legs instead of piercing His side for His remaining blood to drain from His body? Such deaths could not have been a sacrifice for us. Nor would scoffers be compelled to acknowledge that His suffering was consummate.

It took centuries for science to grasp the biblical truth that the life is in the blood, even though the Bible put forth this truth 1400 years before Jesus lived, in Leviticus 17:14: "For the life of all flesh is the blood." Not until sixteen centuries after Christ shed His blood was the circulation of blood understood. George Washington was bled four times when suffering with a sore throat, which hastened his death, though it is said that he had a Bible at his bedside. Nothing was known about different types of blood until 1900. There was no blood bank in America until 1937. Now blood transfusions are saving scores of lives, but transfused blood is contaminating 30,000 Americans with debilitating hepatitis and causing 3000 deaths annually.[1]

Yes, there is power in the blood. But only in the flawless, sanctified blood of Christ is the power of eternal life.

What Is Death?

Today man is confused as to what death is. He has evolved definitions according to his finite intellect: when the heart stops beating; when the lungs stop pumping; when certain cells die and are not replaced; when all human traits are lost without hope of recovery; when spontaneous brain functions irreversibly cease. As man increases the life span, new definitions are required. One man's heart stopped beating and he was pronounced dead five times during open-heart surgery.

The biblical definition is constant. Solomon said the spirit returns to God who gave it (Eccles. 12:7). James said the body without the spirit is dead (James 2:26). The Gospels tell us that Jesus gave up His spirit when He died on the cross.

Doctors, lawyers, clergymen and bereaved are sometimes confused as to whether maintaining heartbeats and breathing by artificial means is an ethical mandate or a defiant interference with God's appointed timing. Dag Hammarskjold, Secretary-General of the United Nations who died in a plane crash on a peace mission, had written in his scrapbook, "Do not seek death. Death will find you. But seek the road which makes death a fulfillment."[2]

When I reach a point beyond recovery I wouldn't trade being ushered into God's presence for all of the organ transplants, intravenous nourishment, lung pumping, transfusions, pills, compassionate doctors and nurses and hospital beds in the catalogue; for I have found the road to fulfillment and do not fear the gate through which I must pass.

The Bible carries us beyond any of those finite definitions of death. The apostle Paul wrote that to depart and be with Christ is gain (Phil. 1:21,23). He told the Christians at Corinth, "We are confident, I say, and willing rather to be absent from the body, and be present with the Lord" (2 Cor. 5:8). Jesus said, "He that heareth my word, and believeth on him that sent me, hath everlasting life, and shall not come into condemnation; but is passed from death unto life" (John 5:24).

We can be confident that we shall have a house eternal in the heavens, not made by hands (see 2 Cor. 5:1). There a welcome awaits us; for the Psalmist has said, "Precious in the sight of the Lord is the death of his saints" (Ps. 116:15).

THE GATE KEEPER

"Death, I have glimpsed your shadow many times,
Now it looms larger, nearer; but no fear
Have I, for you are the keeper of the gate
That opens to my Father's house. Not here,

But only at your gate is entrance found;
And none but you can open it for me.
For you alone, Friend Death, possess the key.

"How could I dread your coming? For I know—
I have assurance from my Father's word—
That greater joy than earth can give or show
Awaits me: 'Eye hath not seen, nor ear heard,
Neither hath entered into the heart of man
The things God hath prepared'—prepared for me!
How could I, then, aught else than happy be?

"I wait with patience, Death, till you shall come
To firmly yet gently take my hand.
Whether you lead up rugged hills of pain
Or through the peaceful dark, at your command
I shall walk with you unafraid. I know
That you will open wide for me the gate
Where love and joy unspeakable await."
                    —Stella Osgood Humphrey[3]

Footnotes

1. Senator Lou Cusanovich, "Report from Sacramento," May 10, 1973.
2. Hammarskjold, Dag, *Markings* (New York, N.Y.: Alfred A. Knopf, Inc., 1964), p. 159.
3. English faculty member of Baylor University, Waco, Texas, who passed away in February 1966. Used by permission of the *Baylor Line*, alumni magazine.

SOME OPPORTUNITIES FOR VOLUNTEER CHRISTIAN SERVICE

BAPTIST WORLD ALLIANCE, 1628 Sixteenth St., N.W., Washington, D.C. 20008.
A fellowship of 95 Baptist Conventions around the world.

CAMPUS CRUSADE FOR CHRIST, INTERNATIONAL, Arrowhead Springs, San Bernardino, Ca. 92404.
Interdenominational and evangelical.
Short or long term service
Abroad: Doctors, dentists, nurses, teachers, and other workers, sent out in teams.
United States: Accountants, auditors, carpenters, electricians, management, mass media, office personnel, painters, plumbers, switchboard operators.

174

CHRISTIAN SERVICE CORPS, 1509 Sixteenth St., N.W., Washington, D.C. 20036.

Interdenominational and evangelical. Patterned after the U. S. Peace Corps. U. S. and abroad.

Term: Two years. Training in U. S. precedes service. Age limits: 18 to 70 years of age.

Service needs: Agriculture, animal husbandry, arts and crafts, Braille, business, clerical, clothing, construction, communication, deaf interpreters, dental, engineers, house parents, literacy, medical, musicians, printers, social workers, teachers, writers.

CONSERVATIVE BAPTIST FOREIGN MISSION SOCIETY, Personnel Dept., Box 5, Wheaton, Ill. 60187.

Career, short and long-term.

Work is classified under these headings in their free brochure, "I Am a Servant": evangelism, education, communication, business, medicine, linguistics, support, and others.

CONSERVATIVE BAPTIST HOME MISSION SOCIETY, Box 828, Wheaton, Ill. 60187.

Short or long-term.

Service needs: Builders, literacy, office work, radio engineers, teachers.

EVANGELICAL FOREIGN MISSIONS ASSOCIATIONS, 100 Western Union Building, 1405 G Street, N.W., Washington, D.C. 20005.

An association of 66 denominational and nondenominational agencies, including Far East Broadcasting Co., The Navigators, and World Vision. Serves 130 mission fields. Operates Universal Travel Service. Write for free brochures.

GOSPEL RECORDINGS, INC., 122 Glendale Blvd., Los Angeles, Ca. 90026.
Evangelical.
Short or long-term.
Service needs: Art, assembling phonettes and cardtalks, carpentry, clerical, engineering, gardening, inspecting, maintenance, sleeving and shipping records.

INTERDENOMINATIONAL FOREIGN MISSION ASSOCIATION, P. O. Box 395, Wheaton, Ill. 60187.
Fellowship of 47 nondenominational foreign mission societies and groups, including Gospel Recordings, Pocket Testament League, and Far East Broadcasting Co.
Write for free brochure, *Opportunities to Serve the Lord Jesus Christ on the Mission Fields of the World.*

LAOS, INC., 4920 Piney Branch Road, N.W., Washington, D.C. 20011.
Ecumenical. Field: Third world.
Terms: One month to two years.
Skills needed: Agriculture, community development, construction, cooking, dentistry, education, mechanics, medicine, office work. Operates on belief one must see

and know people of other cultures for proper perspective of Christian beneficences.

LAUBACH LITERACY, INC., Box 131, Syracuse, New York 13210.
Interdenominational.
Part or full-time: Short or preferably long-term.
Service needs: "Each one teach one" tutors; writers to prepare limited vocabulary literature.

NEW TRIBES MISSIONS, Woodsworth, Wisconsin 53194.
Short and long-term.
Fundamental-interdenominational, world wide.
Numerous areas of service.

RESOURCE SYSTEM FOR PEOPLE IN MISSIONS, Room 133, 475 Riverside Drive, New York, N.Y. 10027.
United Presbyterian.

SHORT TERMS ABROAD, P.O. Box 575, Downers Grove, Ill. 60515.
Represents 163 evangelical agencies, including Campus Crusade, Wycliffe Bible Translators, and Indian missions in the United States.
Terms: A few weeks to two years.
Services needed: 134 job titles classified under aviation, administration, church planting, communication,

construction, engineering, evangelism, education, librarians, mechanics, transportation.

SOUTHERN BAPTIST FOREIGN MISSION BOARD, Box 6597, 3805 Monument Ave., Richmond, Va. 23230.
Short and long term.

Service needs: Appliance repairmen, automobile mechanics, construction, repair and maintenance of buildings, house parents, personal evangelism, teachers.

Mr. William Eugene Grubbs, consultant on "Laymen Overseas," states: "We have more volunteers from the churches of the Southern Baptist Convention than we are able to place at present. . . . We anticipate that in several years we will be commissioning a large para-missionary force made up of volunteer lay people serving for various periods of time."

WORLD MISSION TOURS, Box 515, Miami Springs, Fla. 33166.
Short-term work tours.

Fields of service: Africa, Bolivia, Guatemala, Haiti, Honduras.

Services: Construction, dental, evangelical, medical, music, etc.

WYCLIFFE BIBLE TRANSLATORS, INC., Huntington Beach, Ca. 92648.
Short or long terms.

Field and services: Worldwide and varied.

BIBLIOGRAPHY

Books

Armour, Richard. *Going Like Sixty.* McGraw-Hill Book Co., Inc., New York, N.Y., 1974.

Bauer, W. W., Editor. *Today's Health Guide.* American Medical Association, 535 North Dearborn St., Chicago, Ill. 60610.

Boucheron, Pierre. *How to Enjoy Life After Sixty.* New York, N.Y.: Archer House, Inc., 1959.

Bronterman, Robert. *The Complete Estate Planning Guide.* New York, N.Y. The New American Library, 1301 Avenue of the Americas 10019.

Celebrezze, Chairman, President's Council on Aging, *The Older American.* Washington, D.C.: U.S. Government Printing Office, 1963.

Corlett, D. Shelby. *Retirement Is What You Make of It.* Anderson, Ind.: Warner Press, Inc. 1973.

179

Doyle, Dr. Patrick J. *How to Travel the World and Stay Healthy.* Washington, D.C., Acropolis Press, 1969.

Engle, Lyle K. *The Complete Book of Mobile Home Living.* New York, Arco Publishing Co., 1973.

Frederick, Leland, and Cooley, Lee. *The Retirement Trap.* Garden City, N.Y.: Doubleday and Co., 1965.

Gill, Donald R. *Live, Christian, Live!* Glendale, Ca.: Regal Books, 1971.

Hammarskjold, Dag. *Markings,* New York: Alfred A. Knopf, 1964.

Haggai, John Edmund. *How to Win Over Worry,* Grand Rapids, Mich.: Zondervan Publishing House, 1972.

Hilton, Conrad. *Be My Guest.* Englewood Cliffs, N.J.: Prentice-Hall, Inc., 1957.

Larson, Bruce. *No Longer Strangers.* Waco, Texas: Word Books, 1971.

Legler, Henry. *How to Make the Rest of Your Life the Best of Your Life.* New York, N.Y.: Simon and Schuster, 1967.

Lovett, C.S. *Jesus Wants You Well.* Baldwin Park, Ca.: Personal Christianity, 1973.

Lowman, Dr. Charles Leroy. *Exercises for the Mature Adult.* Los Angeles, Ca.: C. C. Thomas, 1973 (2400 S. Flower St. 90007).

Malloy, Michael T. *The Art of Retirement.* Silver Spring, Maryland: National Observer News Series, 1968.

Margolius, Sidney. *Your Personal Guide to Successful Retirement.* New York, N.Y.: Random House, 1969.

Mow, Anna B. *Who's Afraid of Birthdays?* Philadelphia, Pa.: J. P. Lippincott Co., 1969.

Otte, Elmer. *Welcome Retirement.* St. Louis, Mo.: Concordia Publishing House, 1974.

Parsons, Martin. *Toward Senior Years.* Chicago, Ill.: Moody Press, 1966.

Pitkin, Walter B. *Life at Forty.* New York, N.Y.: McGraw-Hill Book Co., Inc., 1934.

Ross, Sidney Scott. *How to Enjoy Your Later Years.* New York, N.Y.: Grossett and Dunlap, 1962.

Shedd, Charles W. *The Fat Is in Your Head.* Waco, Texas: Word Inc.

Stonecypher, D. D. Jr. *Getting Older and Staying Younger.* New York, N.Y.: W. W. Norton & Co., 500 Fifth Ave.

Stott, John R. W. *Understanding the Bible.* Glendale, Ca.: Regal Books, 1972.

Taylor, Eric. *Stay 39 Forever.* New York, Arco Publishing Co., 1973.

Vischner, A. L. *On Growing Old.* Boston, Mass., translated from German by Gerald Onn, Houghton Mifflin Co., 1967.

Wagner, C. Peter. *Stop the World! I Want to Get On.* Glendale, Ca.: Regal Books, 1974.

Ware, George. *The New Guide to Happy Retirement.* New York, N.Y.: Crown Publishers, Inc., 1968.

Watkins, Grace V. *Beyond the Middle Years.* Anderson, Ind.: Warner Press, 1961.

Whitman, Virginia. *Around the Corner from Sixty.* Chicago, Ill.: Moody Press, 1967.

Williams, Arthur. *Recreation in the Senior Years.* New York, N.Y.: Associated Press, 1962.

Periodicals

AARP NEWS BULLETIN, American Association of Retired Persons, 1225 Connecticut Ave., N.W., Washington, D.C. 20036

AGING, U.S. Department of Health, Education and Welfare, Administration on Aging, Supt. of Documents, Washington, D.C. 20402

LIFE AND HEALTH, M.D. Monthly, 6856 Eastern Ave., N.W., Washington, D.C. 20012

MODERN MATURITY, AARP, 215 Long Beach Blvd., Long Beach, Ca. 90802

NRTA JOURNAL, National Retired Teachers Association, 701 North Montgomery Street, Ojai, Ca. 93023

NRTA NEWS BULLETIN, 1225 Connecticut Ave., Washington, D.C. 20036

RETIREMENT LIVING, 150 East 58th Street, New York, N.Y. 10022

Booklets and Pamphlets

(Free or low-cost. Subject to price changes or discontinuance.)

Bernard, Lee. *A Guide to Your Christian Will.* Christian Freedom Foundation, Inc., 7960 Crescent Ave., Buena Park, CA, 90620.

Morgan, Ernest. *A Manual of Simple Burial.* Burnsville, N.C. 28714. Celo Press.

Randolph, Abigail Graves. *Growing Older! But How?* Upper Room Christian Family Series, 1908 Grand Ave., Nashville, Tenn. 37203.

Bicycle Clubs Directory and Other Stuff, Bicycle Clubs of America, Inc., 122 East 42nd St., New York, N.Y. 10017.

Consumers Guide to Understand Pensions, Penna Insurance Dept., Finance Building, Harrisburg, Pa. 17120. (Free)

Management and Welfare Pensions Report, Public Document Room, U.S. Dept. of Labor, Washington, D.C. 20216. (Free)

Osteoarthritis, A Handbook for Patients, Arthritis Foundation, 1212 Avenue of the Americas, New York, N.Y. 10036. (Free)

Pensions, Information, Travelers Ins. Co., 1 Tower Square, Hartford, Conn. 06115. (Free)

Saltman, Jules, *Light on Your Feet,* Pamphlet No. 345A. Public Affairs Committee, 381 Park Avenue South, New York, N.Y. 10016. (35¢)

The Fitness Challenge in the Later Years, Consumer Product Information Center of General Services Administration, Pueblo, Colo. 81009. (55¢)

Thinking About a Nursing Home? American Nursing Home Assn., 1200 Fifteenth St., N.W., Washington, D.C. 20005. (Free)

The Fitness Challenge in the Later Years, U.S. Dept.

183

of HEW Pub. No. (SRS) 1972, Washington, D.C. 20802. (55¢)
Pamphlets on foot care, American Podiatry Association, 20 Chevy Chase Circle, N.W., Washington, D.C. 20015. (Free)

AARP-NRTA booklets free to members, 215 Long Beach Blvd., Long Beach, CA 90802
Your Retirement Anti-Crime Guide
Your Retirement Consumer Guide
Your Retirement Food Guide
Your Retirement Health Guide
Your Retirement Hobby Guide
Your Retirement Home Guide
Your Retirement Job Guide
Your Retirement Legal Guide
Your Retirement Moving Guide
Your Retirement Pet Guide
Your Retirement Safety Guide

Action for Independent Maturity (AIM) for ages 50 to 65, booklets free to members, 1225 Connecticut Ave., N.W., Washington, D.C. 20036
Getting the Most Out of Leisure Time
How to Build a Rewarding Second Career
How to Make Your Money Work Harder for You
How to Pick a Hobby to Add a New Dimension to Your Life
How to Stay in Tip-top Health After 50
How to Use Legal Help in Planning Your Retirement

Metropolitan Life Insurance Co. free booklets; Community Health Affairs, 600 Stockton St., San Francisco, CA 94120

Four Steps to Weight Control

Stress

Your Health and Your Driving

Booklets available from Superintendent of Documents, U.S. Government Printing Office, Washington, D.C. 20402

Are You Planning on Living the Rest of Your Life? AoA 803 40¢

Cerebral Vascular Disease and Strokes, PHS 513 20¢

Food Guide for Older Folks, Dept. of Agr. 9-17 free

Guide to Budgeting for the Retired Couple, 0100-1518 10¢

Handle Yourself with Care, DHEW 72-20805 30¢

How to Buy Canned and Frozen Vegetables, Home & Garden 167 30¢

Keeping Food Safe to Eat, Homemakers' Guide G-162 free

Let's Find Isolation, DHEW 72-20129 30¢

Little Strokes, Pub. Health Service 698 10¢

The Fitness Challenge in the Later Years, DHEW 72-20802 30¢

You, the Law and Retirement, OA 72-20800 25¢

Retirement Living kit $6 or $1.25 each. 99 Garden St. Marion, Ohio 43306

Health and Your Retirement